Passionate Fictions

Passionate Fictions:
Gender, Narrative, and
Violence in
Clarice Lispector

Marta Peixoto

University of Minnesota Press
Minneapolis
London

Copyright 1994 by the Regents of the University of Minnesota

Chapter 2, "Female Power in *Family Ties,*" first appeared as "*Family Ties:* Female Development in Clarice Lispector," in *The Voyage In: Fictions of Female Development,* edited by Elizabeth Abel, Marianne Hirsch, and Elizabeth Langland, copyright 1983 by the Trustees of Dartmouth College, reprinted by permission of the University Press of New England. Chapter 5, "Rape and Textual Violence," first appeared as "Rape and Textual Violence in Clarice Lispector," in *Rape and Representation,* edited by Lynn Higgins and Brenda Silver, copyright 1991 by Columbia University Press, New York, reprinted by permission of the publisher.

All rights reserved. No part of this publication may be reproduced, stored in a retrieval system, or transmitted, in any form or by any means, electronic, mechanical, photocopying, recording, or otherwise, without the prior written permission of the publisher.

Published by the University of Minnesota Press
2037 University Avenue Southeast, Minneapolis, MN 55455-3092

Library of Congress Cataloging-in-Publication Data

Peixoto, Marta.
   Passionate fictions : gender, narrative, and violence in Clarice
Lispector / Marta Peixoto.
     p. cm.
   Includes bibliographical references (p.) and index.
   ISBN 0-8166-2158-6 (acid-free). — ISBN 0-8166-2159-4 (pb. :
acid -free)
    1. Lispector, Clarice—Criticism and interpretation. 2. Women in
literature. 3. Sex role in literature. 4. Violence in literature. I.
Title
PQ9697.L585Z84 1994
869.3—dc20   93-29690
                                                                                                                             CIP

The University of Minnesota is an
equal-opportunity educator and employer.

For Jim, Daniel, Thomas, and Mariana

Contents

Acknowledgments ix
Introduction xi
1. The Young Artist and the Snares of Gender 1
2. Female Power in *Family Ties* 24
3. The Nurturing Text in Hélène Cixous and Clarice Lispector 39
4. A Woman Writing: Fiction and Autobiography in
    The Stream of Life and *The Stations of the Body* 60
5. Rape and Textual Violence 82
Afterword: The Violence of a Heart 100
Notes 103
Bibliography 109
Index 113

Acknowledgments

Over the many years it has taken me to write this book I have profited in ways I cannot even measure from conversations with students and colleagues here and in Brazil, and from the responses of audiences to the lectures I have given on Lispector. I am also very grateful for the institutional support I have received in the form of several grants and fellowships from Yale University (a Whitney Griswold Faculty Research Grant, a summer travel grant from the Yale Center for International and Area Studies, and a Senior Faculty Fellowship) and a sabbatical leave from New York University. I would also like to thank the staff at the Arquivo-Museu de Literatura at the Fundação Casa de Rui Barbosa in Rio de Janeiro, especially Eliane Vasconcellos, who allowed me to look at materials she was still engaged in cataloguing for the Clarice Lispector Archive.

Two sections of this book were published previously in somewhat different forms. Chapter 2 appeared in *The Voyage In: Fictions of Female Development*, edited by Elizabeth Abel, Marianne Hirsch, and Elizabeth Langland. A version of chapter 5 appeared first in the proceedings of a conference at the University of Texas at Austin, *Transformations of Literary Language in Latin American Literature*, edited by K. David Jackson. Later, another version was published in *Rape and Representation*, edited by Lynn Higgins and Brenda Silver. I thank the editors for their invitations and helpful comments. Participation in those projects first made me see that there would be an audience for a book of this kind in English.

Many friends and colleagues have provided invaluable comments on drafts of this book over the years. My greatest debt is to my husband, Jim Irby, always my first reader, for his numerous and patient readings of the manuscript in its many versions, for his attention to details, his insistence on precision and clarity, and his many helpful suggestions. Marianne Hirsch also read the entire manuscript, some sections in more than one draft. I thank her for her generosity, her many thoughtful comments, and, not least, her contagious enthusiasm for intellectual projects. (For other projects, too.) Sylvia Molloy has been a most supportive friend and critic throughout the writing of this book; her insightful reading of the manuscript clarified some of its latent articulations, allowing me in turn to sharpen them in the final version. Elizabeth Abel provided unfailing friendship and brought to sections of the book pertinent questions and a keen editorial eye. I would also like to thank the anonymous readers for their thought-provoking comments; I hope that my attempts to respond to their objections have improved the book.

Although many friends offered me their help during the writing of this book, when family and professional urgencies clashed more than once, I owe special thanks to Jane Coppock, whose presence and cheerfulness were enormously heartening to me and my children. And finally, although my sons, Daniel and Thomas, have not exactly helped with this project, I am grateful to them nonetheless for keeping me busy and happy with challenges of another sort.

Introduction

Cuando a la casa del lenguaje se le vuela el tejado y las palabras no guarecen, yo hablo.

[When the house of language has its roof blown off and words do not shelter, I speak.]

Alejandra Pizarnik,
"Fragmentos para dominar el silencio"
(Fragments to overcome silence)

I

Clarice Lispector might, but for a twist of fate, have become a writer in the English language. She was born in the small Ukrainian village of Tchetchelnik: a necessary stop for her birth along the way when her parents, Ukrainian Jews, had set out to emigrate, not yet knowing their destination. They had relatives both in the United States and in Brazil and for a while hesitated between North and South America (Moreira 1981).[1] Arriving in Brazil at age two months, Lispector came to consider the country and its language her own. Like other major Brazilian writers, Lispector looked upon the Portuguese language with some melancholy, witnessing the meager audience it could afford her: *o túmulo do pensamento*, "the tomb of one's thought," she called it in one essay where she measures the advantages and disadvantages of writing in Portuguese (*DW* 134). At the time of

Lispector's death in 1977, only three of her books had been translated into French or English. How astonished she would be to witness the recent upsurge of translations of her work: most of her fourteen books of fiction are now available in English, French, and Spanish, and several have been translated into other languages.

For Lispector, writing in Portuguese offered a challenge that she describes in the same essay:

> It's not easy. It's not malleable. And, since thought has not worked upon it profoundly, it tends to lack subtleties, and to kick back at those who boldly dare to transform it into a language of feeling and alertness. And love. The Portuguese language offers a real challenge to any writer. Especially to those who write removing from things and people the first layer of superficiality.
>
> Sometimes it reacts when confronted by a more complicated process of thought. Sometimes it takes fright at the unexpectedness of a phrase. I love to handle it—as I loved to ride a horse and guide it with the reins, sometimes slowly, sometimes at a gallop. (*DW* 134)

Lispector's mode of writing would have required a struggle with any language, just as it did with established literary genres, especially in her later work. Since publication of her first book, *Perto do coração selvagem* (1944; *Near to the Wild Heart*), critics have recognized a distinctive contribution in Lispector's original, often strange language, dense with paradoxes, unusual phrases, and abstract formulations that tease and elude the rational intelligence. João Guimarães Rosa, an acknowledged master of twentieth-century Brazilian fiction and a Joycean innovator in language himself, told an interviewer that "every time he read one of her novels he learned many new words and rediscovered new uses for the ones he already knew" (Rodriguez Monegal 1966, 1001). The second lesson Rosa derived is perhaps more to the point: Lispector's linguistic inventiveness centers not so much on the lexical level, on the use of unusual words or neologisms (in which Rosa himself excelled), but rather on syntactical contortions and strange juxtapositions, creating semantic pressures that unsettle the meaning of words and concepts.

Although Lispector preferred to think of herself as a writer unmodified by the adjective "female,"[2] issues of gender are crucial in her work. This book, which takes as its intellectual and theoretical ground recent feminist critical approaches, studies the pressures Lispector brings to bear on the fixities of gender and the routines of narrative, pressures similar to those that agitate her language. My project is to study the nexus between gender, narrative, and violence, an aspect of Lispector's work that has not been sufficiently recognized, even by her feminist critics.

The female dimension of Lispector's writing has been discussed by many critics. Hélène Cixous finds in her texts a feminine libidinal economy, revealing itself in openness and generosity, or gentle, identificatory movements toward objects and beings, an interpretation I question in chapter 3. Other critics find a feminist *parti pris* in Lispector's fiction, and read in various of her texts a critique of social and narrative structures that confine women. Although I do not disagree with this position, I attempt to include her defense of women and the feminine in a more encompassing perspective, charting what I see as a conflictive course in Lispector's texts, where a feminist happy ending seldom occurs. Lispector and her female protagonists engage in work that Teresa de Lauretis identifies as necessary for women as producers of meaning: "a continued and sustained work with and against narrative, in order to represent not just the power of female desire but its duplicity and ambivalence. . . . The real task is to enact the contradictions of female desire and of women as social subjects, in terms of narrative" (de Lauretis 1984, 156). It is in the texts with a metafictional dimension, where the protagonist is a self-reflexive writer, that I find the best examples of Lispector's fierce struggle with gender and narrative, which produces a formal and thematic violence. Challenging limits and courting excess, Lispector invokes a Dionysian force in her attempt to question and disrupt the fixity of gender, of established genres and narrative forms, and to authorize a writing that not only represents women, but also often claims to be itself moved by powers especially accessible to women.

"I feel in me a subterranean violence, a violence that only surfaces in the act of writing," affirms the female writer-protagonist of Lispector's posthumous novel *Um sopro de vida* (1978; *A Breath of Life,* 53). In the texts I choose for analysis, I find many manifestations of violence articulated with gender and narrative. There is, first, a mimetic violence: the representation of dominating or aggressive interactions between men and women, often set in the family or placed within larger systems of social and even racial oppression. In her refusal to see women simply as innocent victims, Lispector runs counter to a major tendency in feminist thought that Jessica Benjamin also opposes: the construction of "the problem of domination as a drama of female vulnerability victimized by male aggression" (Benjamin 1988, 9). Lispector observes not only the sufferings of women under patriarchy, but also their sometimes devious access to an aggressive power; in larger terms, she writes about the multiple violences unavoidably present in biologic, psychic, and social life.

Lispector's texts also exemplify and at times metafictionally discuss what we might call a narrative violence. In her writing of the 1970s, the struggle with narrative that Lispector's work foregrounds includes a conflictive juxtaposition of genres: she uses autobiography to call into question the supposed self-sufficiency of fiction and she uses fiction to mask and disrupt the autobiographical impulse. Also in the 1970s she experiments with and parodies the themes and strategies of popular fiction. By means of these parodies Lispector casts an ironic light on her own practice elsewhere of finely wrought, introspective fictions of a kind that modernism had canonized as high art. In the 1970s Lispector also questions most sharply the uncomfortable aggressions contained in the narrative pact. These include not only the age-old entanglement of narrative with the representation of suffering, but also the inward-turned and almost sacrificial suffering of the author that narrative may require. "Can it be that it's my painful task to imagine in the flesh the truth that no one wants to face?" Lispector's narrator asks in *A hora da estrela* (1977; *The Hour of the Star; HS* 56). Lispector's text ensures that the writer's pain is shared by the reader. A writing that insistently imagines disturbances of the psyche as well as painful transgressions of the social order and of the routines of fiction will necessarily be less than comfortable for the reader. The reader Lispector's fiction sometimes implies and at other times addresses must be startled, seduced, or even dominated in an uneasy engagement with her text.

Some of the aggressive aspects of Lispector's narratives can be read as gendered, along the lines elaborated by feminist narratologists and film theorists (Laura Mulvey, Teresa de Lauretis, Tania Modleski). These critics have reflected on the relation of spectatorship to gender ideology and on the oppressiveness for women of a narrative based on "a male Oedipal logic" (de Lauretis 1984, 152) that tends to exclude women from the position of subject. In another critique of the assimilation of the Oedipus model into cultural discourses, Jessica Benjamin discusses "its updated, subtler form": "a version of male dominion that works through the cultural ideal, the ideal of individuality and rationality that survives even the waning of paternal authority and the rise of more equitable family structures" (Benjamin 1988, 173). In her passionate fictions, Lispector undermines the authority of reason, which she repeatedly construes as a version of male domination, both in her characters and plots (or their erasure) and in the very texture of her dense, oxymoronic language with its tendency toward self-contradiction and the dissolution of logical sense. Throughout her work, Lispector searches for alternate sources of power and organization. The intuitive and the improvisatory, which she associates with the feminine, replace rational construction and logical progression in the unfolding of her fictions; they also challenge the boundaries, separateness, and coherence of the subject.

"As if in a retort to the Cartesian dictum 'I think, therefore I am' . . . , [Lispector] asks herself permanently 'I who narrate, who am I?'" (Nunes 1982, 21). To answer this question in her fiction—or perhaps to avoid answers and persist in the questioning—author, narrator, and characters engage in vertiginous doublings and mirrorings. In one of her autobiographical pieces, she describes this exchange between self and other:

Before, I had wanted to be other people to understand that which is not me. I then realized that I had already been others and that it was easy. My greatest experience would be to be the inner core of others, and the inner core of others was me. (*DW* 508)

In an earlier version of this fragment from *A legião estrangeira* (1964; *The Foreign Legion*), Lispector wrote "the other of others" in place of "the inner core of others," pointing up the extent to which otherness inhabits the space of an inner core where identity and alterity become inextricably enmeshed. "My greatest experience," the earlier version reads, "would be to be the other of others, and the other of others was me" (*FL* 119). A disunified, inconsistent subjectivity, unknown to itself, is constantly invading and being invaded by others, in a continuous exchange that forms and dissolves in the words of so many of her texts.

This exchange between self and other at the heart of Lispector's fiction is not peaceful, but instead is charged with double-edged violent forces. The passionate aspect of Lispector's writing, which many critics have noted and which Lispector herself stresses—in the title of *A paixão segundo G.H.* (1964; *The Passion according to G.H.*), for example—involves not only the quest for positive connections, as in the passion of love, or the intense introspection of her characters, who seek contact with truths that reason cannot fathom or represent. It also includes the sacrificial impulse that sparks her fictional imagination: a *via crucis*, with its Christian resonances of suffering in place of and for the sake of another, a process that does not always follow ethical and moral precepts, and that may be required of the characters as well as suffered by their author.

In a closing autobiographical piece in *The Foreign Legion*, Lispector describes a strong, irrational response to the police shooting of the dangerous Brazilian outlaw Mineirinho, who "had murdered far too often" (*FL* 213). He has infringed the commandment "Thou shalt not kill," yet to her dismay she cannot accept the justice of his death:

> That commandment is my greatest guarantee: so do not kill me, for I do not wish to die, and do not let me kill, for to have killed would cast me into eternal darkness.
>
> This is the commandment. But while I listen to the first and the second shot with a sense of relief and reassurance, the third shot makes me alert, the fourth leaves me anxious, the fifth and sixth cover me with shame, I hear the seventh and eighth while my heart beats with horror, at the ninth and tenth my mouth is trembling, at the eleventh shot, I am appalled and invoke the name of God, and at the twelfth I call for my brother. The thirteenth shot kills me—because I am the other. Because I want to be the other. (*FL* 213)

The meditation that follows probes the injustices of justice, the guilt for her own violence that she allowed him to carry for her, and the permeable boundaries between the virtuous and the sinful. In this book I argue that a similar vigilant alertness to inter- and intrasubjective violence shapes many of Lispector's narratives.

Here this alertness presented literally as the wrenching reversal from identification with the killer to identification with the victim, although the victim is a killer and his killers are the police. Her self-reflexive authors, especially in the later narratives, are uneasily aware of contradictory masochistic and sadistic investments in the fate of their characters. Lispector echoes their concerns in an interview of 1969, during which the interviewer reports: "About her characters [Lispector] only says she is sorry she places them at times in terrible situations, but that is her way, a harsh way, inflexible, almost pitiless" (Gorga Filho 1969). My readings of Lispector's fiction point up the contradictory forces that strip her words of their power to shelter and, to their discomfort but also to their illumination, expose her readers to the storm.

II

As is often the case with modern Latin American writers, even long after their deaths, no book-length biography of Lispector exists.[3] While living abroad, she wrote many letters to her sisters and Brazilian friends, who served informally as her literary agents. Fragments from twenty-five of the letters to her sisters have been published (Borelli 1981), a small portion of what seems to have been an extensive correspondence. Lispector's talent was recognized immediately upon the publication of her first novel in 1944 (it won a literary prize and received many positive reviews), but only in the 1960s, when she returned permanently to Brazil after fifteen years in Europe and the United States, did she become celebrated in her country. That very celebrity, with its attendant proliferation of interviews (which she claimed to have hated and granted with at times obvious reluctance), complicates considerably the task of getting straight some basic facts about her life.

Lispector was sensitive about certain areas in her personal and literary life, and was not above lying when pressed for information about them. One area was her birth date and early childhood. She was generally believed to have been born in 1925, whereas documents that recently became public reveal her birth date as 1920.[4] Lispector's reason for equivocating may well have been vanity, even literary vanity, in a wish to appear more precocious at the time of her literary debut in 1944. Her wish for privacy about this matter was preserved by her family: her tombstone does not register the date of her birth, only that of her death. (See photograph of Lispector's tombstone in Varin 1987, 220.) To help erase those years, Lispector stated many times that the family settled immediately in Recife, a major port in northeast Brazil, when they actually spent their three initial years in the smaller city of Maceió. Lispector's dating of events in her life, even her children's ages in her later years, is unreliable. Her dating, however, does coincide with external evidence about two major events: her mother, a paralytic for all of Lispector's life, died when her daughter was nine, and at age twelve Lispector moved with her father and two older sisters to Rio de Janeiro. Lispector denied that she ever spoke or understood Russian, but in an interview with her eldest sister, Elisa Lispector, Claire Varin ascertained that Yiddish was spoken at home during Lispector's early years and that the child Clarice understood it even if she never spoke it. The many remaining questions about Lispector's early years, such as the family's economic circumstances (they were very poor, Lispector often said) and their participation, if any, in a community of Jewish immigrants, await answers in a much-needed biography.[5] Elisa Lispector, also a novelist, has written an autobiographical novel, *No exílio* (1948; *In Exile*), which presents a version of those early years, shadowed by their mother's deteriorating health and death. This novel dwells on the family's story as an example of the Jewish diaspora and on the eldest daughter's difficult adaptation to Brazil. It depicts a father passionately concerned with the fate of the Jews in Europe and with the establishment of Israel, and a family that retains Jewish customs.

Another area of privacy for Lispector is her reading, especially when interviewers touch on literary influences and intellectual affiliations. Out of a fear of appearing merely derivative—early reviewers were quick to mention, much to Lispector's distress, the "influences" of James Joyce and Virginia Woolf—she almost always avoided questions about her literary interests, especially current ones, deflecting the issue back to her voracious and chaotic reading during adolescence. At that time she was especially drawn to Dostoyevski, Katherine Mansfield, and Hermann Hesse; she also chose books from lending libraries alphabetically by the author ("So I got to *Crime and Punishment* rather quickly") or by the mere appeal of the title (Lowe 1979, 37). Although at times Lispector contradicts herself, she always claims to have read the writer in question only after writing the book he or she supposedly influenced. In an interview in 1979, for instance, she places her reading of Sartre in 1944 (Colasanti et al. 1988, 300); in another, she insists she had never read or even heard of Sartre until after she had written *A maçã no escuro* (1961; *An Apple in the Dark*) (Lapouge and Pisa 1977, 197). Her wish apparently was to appear as a writer guided only by a dazzling intuition, but she clearly was not, as Olga Borelli (a close friend and author of a memoir about Lispector) has described her, simply "a housewife who wrote novels and short stories" (Borelli 1981, 14). Letters to her sisters during her sixteen years abroad show her preoccupied with methodical reading and sustained, disciplined writing, and often distressed at falling short of her goals. (Excerpts from those letters appear in Borelli 1981, 105-46.) "I haven't written a single line," Lispector complains in a letter of 1946 to one of her sisters, "and this makes me very uneasy. I am always waiting for inspiration with an eagerness that leaves me no peace. I have even come to the conclusion that writing is what I most desire in the world, even more than love" (Borelli 1981, 114).

While attending law school, Lispector worked as a journalist in Rio. In 1943, she married a fellow student who became a diplomat, with whom she lived abroad for the better part of the next fifteen years. In 1959, Lispector returned to Brazil with her two sons, after separating from her husband. She lived comfortably in an apartment facing Leme beach in Rio, supplementing her husband's financial support with income from translations and journalism, including a conventional biweekly women's column written under the pseudonym "Helen Palmer" (tips on fashion, grooming, child rearing, makeup, recipes, advice on keeping a husband interested, warnings to refrain from appearing a *femme savante*).[6] Lispector had friends who were important writers (Fernando Sabino, Rubem Braga, Nélida Piñon, among others), but she did not engage in anything that could be called a literary life. She insisted in almost every interview from the 1960s and 1970s that she was neither an intellectual nor a professional writer (by this she meant that she never kept to a schedule, but wrote only when she felt moved to do so). In 1967, she had to undergo several operations for the serious burns she suffered from a fire in her apartment that almost took her life. Her right hand, although not entirely incapacitated, became permanently impaired. In the last decade of her life she was plagued by despondent moods that, from the evidence of her interviews, were at times acute.[7] She continued to publish until her death from cancer on December 9, 1977, the day before her fifty-seventh birthday.

III

Although Lispector was acclaimed early on as an extraordinary writer, it was not until more than twenty years after the publication of her first novel that a book-length study of her work appeared in Brazil. In that book, Benedito Nunes's erudite and acute readings pointed up the philosophical issues in her work and were instrumental in securing for Lispector a respected position in the canon of Brazilian literature (Nunes 1966). As other critics were to do later, he traced the affinities between the philosophical ideas present in her fiction and those of Heidegger, Kierkegaard, Camus, and Sartre. Other of her early critics analyzed aspects of her style: her use of the epiphany and of rhetorical devices like the internal monologue. More recently, questions of gender, narrative, poststructuralism, and postmodernism have been brought to bear on her text. (See, for instance, Fitz 1987 and 1988b.) Lispector was singled out as one of two Brazilian writers (the other was Guimarães Rosa) belonging to the so-called Boom of Latin American fiction in the 1960s. However, only in the late 1970s and 1980s did she emerge as an object of extensive international attention in the wake of feminist criticism and, perhaps especially, of Hélène Cixous's celebration of her work as a model of *écriture féminine*.

Although ten of Lispector's fourteen books of fiction are currently available in English, criticism of her work in English is still scarce. In addition to a rapidly growing number of articles, there are two books: Earl Fitz's *Clarice Lispector* (1985), an overview of her complete fiction, and Hélène Cixous's transcripts of her seminars on several of Lispector's texts entitled *Reading with Clarice Lispector* (1990).

I will consider representative moments of Lispector's fiction in the following chapters, which are intended primarily as readings of certain texts, a task that is not superfluous in the case of a complex writer whose interpretation is far from exhausted. I hope as well that the paradigms I propose will prove applicable to other of Lispector's works and suggestive in the study of other women writers. My impetus for writing this book derives in part from my responses to other critics of Lispector, mainly from my objections to Hélène Cixous. Some of the information that guided my readings is new to Lispector criticism and was acquired in archival research in Brazil (unpublished letters, personal documents, early drafts of her work, and other papers from Lispector's private files recently made available for consultation).

As I map shifting intersections of gender, narrative, and violence in Lispector's career, I arrange the texts I consider in roughly chronological order. Chapter 1 juxtaposes Lispector's first novel, *Near to the Wild Heart* (1944), and the short story "The Misfortunes of Sofia" (1964), read as fictional portrayals of the developing artist and as meditations on gender and the female writer's vocation. In her presentation of writing as a gendered and violently disquieting enterprise, Lispector comes to a different conclusion in each text on how to bring about the vexed articulation of woman and writing. Whereas the novel describes artistic creation as requiring the ruthless (and joyful) refusal of gendered social roles, the short story shows the young girl discovering that female gender conveys a form of power that can be played to a writer's advantage. In chapter 2, I examine other instances of the conflict-ridden intersection of gender and development that have a less triumphant outcome. The plots of the short stories of *Laços de familia* (1960; *Family Ties*) reveal the plight of women caught in gender roles, whereas the narrative strategies manipulate the reader alternately into sympathy and disdain for them.

Chapter 3 addresses, in somewhat polemic terms, Cixous's influential readings of Lispector from the perspective, not of Lispector's usefulness to Cixous's own theoretical enterprise, as many of her American and European commentators have done, but of Cixous's illumination of Lispector's texts. This reverse direction might seem unwarranted because Cixous is not a conventional critic "at the service" of another author. It is, however, this very appropriation of Lispector, within a rhetoric that celebrates and imitates Lispector's nurturing, nonappropriative gaze, that I wish to point to and question.

Chapter 4 studies two late works that mark a turning point in Lispector's writing: *Água viva* (1973; *The Stream of Life*) and *A via crucis do corpo* (1974; *The Stations of the Body*). The conflictive tensions that earlier were located in her characters' actions and inner lives now also appear in the narrator's questioning of the very fiction she produces. At issue especially are the particularities of a woman's writing: its access to special modes of power, its obligation to uphold icons of femininity such as the nurturing mother, or its freedom to transgress the boundaries of conventional feminine decorum and of genre, especially those that distinguish autobiography from fiction and carefully crafted "artistic" fiction from the more commercially appealing narratives that capitalize on sex and violence.

The concluding chapter was in many ways the point of departure for this book. In studying *The Hour of the Star* (1977), the last text Lispector published before she died, I became aware that it functioned not simply as a work of "social criticism," but rather as a radical questioning of how narrative itself was implicated in structures of domination and victimization. I attempt in this chapter to show a progression in Lispector's work from earlier stories, in which violence against women inheres in social, ideological, and aesthetic structures that somehow minimize and contain it, to a later stage that reveals how the violence inflicted on a particularly forsaken and comically helpless young woman springs from multiple sources. Lispector's broader vision brings out sharply these sources of violence in a way that does not spare either writer or reader.

Although I have chosen for analysis texts in which the questioning of gender, narrative, and violence is explicit, others, such as *The Passion according to G.H.* or the posthumous *A Breath of Life* would, I think, respond to investigations along similar lines. The chapters in this book are not intended, then, as a closed and fixed series, but instead as an opening up of areas of conflict in Lispector's work that have not been sufficiently addressed before. Neither do I want to substitute a "violent" Lispector for the more accepted "philosophical" or "nurturing" one, but rather to bring up for discussion neglected aspects of her texts that are crucial to one of Lispector's main innovations: an inscription of the feminine that is not a sentimental withdrawal from the struggles of power, but is instead an exacerbated sensitivity to their workings and to women's—and writers'—involvement in these struggles, not as passive victims but as active participants. This study calls for a renewed attention to the letter of Lispector's text, to its densities and contradictions, to its tendency toward the ideologically and aesthetically transgressive, to its skill with comic, parodic, and farcical modes. These and other provocative peculiarities of her texts should not be flattened out by too easy an accommodation to dominant theoretical paradigms that neutralize their force; they should be, and no doubt will be, discovered and attended to by other readers for as long as her writing continues to fascinate, question, and disturb us.

1
The Young Artist and the Snares of Gender

Near to the Wild Heart, Clarice Lispector's first novel, published in 1944, is not the work of a seventeen-year-old, as Lispector herself claimed in more than one interview[1] and as critics have often repeated, but a strikingly mature and still precocious novel written by a young woman in her early twenties. We now know that Lispector was born in 1920 and not in 1925, the year she preferred to give as her birth date before altering it further to 1926 and 1927 toward the end of her life.[2] These equivocations, certainly of interest to biographers and literary historians, are pertinent also to the reception of *Near to the Wild Heart*. This novel, perhaps because of its supposedly adolescent composition, has not received the detailed scrutiny devoted to Lispector's later fiction. Yet it is, I believe, one of Lispector's most interesting novels, deserving of closer reading than it has received. Perhaps Lispector's insistence that its composition dated to adolescence was her way of pulling back from her forceful feminist rejection of conventional feminine roles for the protagonist. The first of Lispector's many articulations of the disturbing consequences—for the social status quo and for traditional artistic forms—of women who practice their art, this novel, with extraordinary, perhaps even youthful boldness, proposes an uncompromising and joyful rejection of all the forces that constrain female talent.

As a *Künstlerroman*, this novel encodes in its peculiar structure the development Lispector imagines for a female artist. The protagonist, Joana, from childhood to young womanhood gropes her way toward literary creation, conceived as the untrammeled expression of three faculties she possesses to a marked degree: "feeling," "thinking," and "saying." It is the story of a fierce vocation that

Joana herself only slowly comes to recognize, and of the obstacles it meets in the social roles a young woman is expected to assume and in her own wavering need to conform to them. Whether as dutiful daughter, wife, mother, or lover, a smothering subservience threatens to dull and bury Joana's artistic potential. She considers or enters each of these roles and, by a combination of happy accident and uncompromising independence, discards them all. As Joana's admired teacher tells her when she is still a child, "You are the kind who would kill to be able to flower."[3]

In this fascinating articulation of gender and a writer's vocation, female gender appears as a liability that the young writer must suppress with a cold-blooded willingness to kill. For Joana, that strategic ruthlessness taints with evil the work of the imagination. In Joana, Lispector recasts, from a gender-marked perspective, the romantic notion of the prerogatives of genius and the defiance of the *poète maudit*. Joana takes pride in her transgressions, and seeks the evil she associates with the capacity to create:

> The certainty that I tend toward evil, thought Joana.
> What else could that feeling of restrained force be, ready to explode into violence, that urge to use it with her eyes shut, all of it, with the unbridled confidence of a wild beast? . . .
> She resisted the idea of unleashing this animal someday. . . . No, no, — she repeated to herself — one mustn't be afraid to be creative. (*WH* 16)

This novel posits, then, a young artist as a practitioner of evil. Although she courts evil more in theory than in practice, Joana's acute sensibility is mesmerized by the transgression and violence that help her break out of a circumscribed feminine place. As an adolescent, she overhears a conversation in which her aunt refers to her as a "cold-blooded viper" (*WH* 47). She accepts her fearful new guise, considering it a confirmation of her unknown, unlimited potential: "Ah, one could expect everything from her, the viper, even what appeared strange, the viper, ah, the pain, the painful joy" (*WH* 55).

The utopian freedom from the constraints of gender that Joana achieves at the end of the novel is only a first stage of Lispector's lengthy meditation on gender and female talent that continues throughout her work. I will examine the implications of this initial articulation and offer a reading of the novel that interprets its peculiar oneiric texture and melodramatic plot. I will then consider a short story, written some twenty years later, "The Misfortunes of Sofia" (in *The Foreign Legion*, 1964). This text discloses a nine-year-old girl's recognition of her literary vocation, a discovery that is embedded in the child's belligerent infatuation with her male teacher. This discovery is mediated by an older Sofia, who narrates the story and comments on the convergences of sexual and literary desire, of loving and writing. Here, in an expanded and deeper meditation on writing and violence, the writer appears as temptress and subverter of conventions, who enacts her transgressions in the textual adventure of feeling, thinking, and saying in uncharted territories. For Lispector, writing reenacts the voracious daring of the Fall, sometimes figured in the Paradise-perverting image of the snake. Writing pursues a new knowledge, violating prohibitions designed to maintain the social order, and offers to author and reader alike its inviting, though often bitter, fruit. In both the novel and the later short story, Lispector reinscribes a traditional and misogynist myth by associating woman and snake. Whereas Joana uses the allegiance to evil implicit in this metaphor to protect herself against the traps of femininity that would kill her artist's vocation, Sofia, as we will see, plays the writer as temptress, seducing the reader into her transgressive texts. Through Sofia, Lispector claims for the woman writer a powerful adequacy of the female gender for literary pursuit. If woman is a temptress and writing must tempt us into the arduous subversions a new knowledge requires, what better mediator than a woman's textual snares?

I

In the absence of an omniscient narrator, the narrative of *Near to the Wild Heart* enacts the consciousness of several characters who, by turns, occupy center stage. Yet Joana's subjectivity and development dominate the novel, as Benedito Nunes suggests when he terms it one of Lispector's "monocentric novels" (Nunes 1973, 3). The narrative implicitly admires Joana and confirms her conviction of her own exceptionality. Her transgressions appear necessary, her choices wise, and events beyond her control further her path toward autonomy and creativity. The other characters have remarkably little independence from Joana. Although many are given internal, even lengthy, monologues, they either reflect on Joana—agreeing, in admiration or horror, about her specialness—or provide studied contrasts to her personality. This intense concentration on Joana lends the novel an oneiric texture. As in a dream, all elements refer, ostensibly or covertly, to one subjectivity. The other characters become agents of her inner drama, helpers or opponents of her quest, providers of models or countermodels. Yet the novel is not, of course, a dream, and its fantasies and predicaments belong to a larger social and cultural network. Lispector imagines, with partiality and passionate engagement, how a woman's talent might arise and assert itself in a patriarchal setting. What does it take for a woman to become an artist? What obstacles will she encounter? What price will she pay?

One problem in the interpretation of this novel arises from what we might call the disjunction of background and foreground. Why the melodramatic plot—deaths, betrayals, love encounters, triangles, and separations—when the narrative focuses on intense first- and third-person monologues occurring in moments of solitude? The plot is eventful, but it takes place offstage. Only on a few occasions is the dramatic action furthered by means of confrontational dialogues. Yet painful encounters and separations form the novel's context. Joana, the motherless child of a widowed father, at first enjoys his love and indulgence. After his sudden death, she is taken in by an aunt and uncle, but her disinterest in daughterly affection makes her an uncomfortable stepchild. Following a shoplifting incident, she is sent off to a boarding school. Later her marriage to a law professor entails a complicated arrangement of double infidelities, a separation, and a final, triumphant voyage, during which Joana lives out the promise of the Joycean title and epigraph: "He was alone. He was unheeded, happy, near to the wild heart of life" (*Portrait of the Artist as a Young Man*). Structured as juxtaposed episodes connected only implicitly, in what Roberto Schwarz calls "a constellation where moments shine side by side without close articulation" (Schwarz 1965, 39), the novel is divided into two parts: the first alternates between scenes from Joana's childhood and her adulthood; the second presents moments of her life as a young woman in a mostly linear progression.

Critics of this novel have dealt with the disjunction of outer eventfulness and subjective reflection by claiming, with remarkable unanimity, that only the inner realm matters. "The external events are few and insignificant" (Nunes 1973, 3); "the facts of the book do not matter" (Lins 1963, 189); or, as Berta Waldman affirms more emphatically: "Indeed, the 'fabula' of this novel hardly matters. . . . One could even say that Joana has no biography, so tenuous is the organization of the facts of her life" (Waldman 1983, 28). I would argue, however, that those facts do matter. In them Lispector encodes the problematic participation by Joana and the female artist in the social order. If, as I propose, we read the novel as a *Künstlerroman*, we must grant those facts an importance that many critics deny. As a woman artist, Joana pursues her vocation against events, willed or accidental, that demand from her other allegiances. And if, moreover, we read the novel as a sort of psychomachia, an enactment of Joana's inner drama, characters and events take on additional significance as possibilities that Joana seeks or rejects in herself.

Most critics, from the early reviews on, point to the autobiographical dimension of this novel—Joana "is" Clarice Lispector—yet offer little credit to the protagonist as a developing writer.[4] Roberto Schwarz, for instance, comments:

> One frequently feels that Joana is on the brink of artistic creation, that her reflections and sensations tend toward organization. The novel becomes poignant when the protagonist realizes that she will speak, that her impressions, her love, her most intimate being will become condensed in words; what her mouth utters is a sweet murmuring of disconnected syllables, a purely expressive, elementary language, anterior to the possibility of communication. (Schwarz 1965, 41)

The examples of Mallarmé and Joyce, and Guimarães Rosa in Brazil, as well as

Julia Kristeva's major studies of the elements in language and literature that are heterogeneous to sense and signification, remind us that Joana's preverbal, creative babble is indeed relevant to an artistic apprenticeship. Lispector, through Joana and other of her writer characters, often represents the vertiginous moment of creation, in which conflicting forces flow in currents and countercurrents through a divided subject. In addition to moments of "sweet murmuring," the novel includes many scenes in which Joana engages in narrative and poetic invention. The representation of Joana's artistic talent is worked out in compelling detail, depicting not only her power to say but also the social dynamics that govern instances of her saying: the performance of her text.

How does gender function in Lispector's portrait of the incipient artist? To answer this question we should examine the recurring Oedipal structures in Joana's tangled relations with the other characters. If we focus on the "facts" of Joana's life, we will see that the plot, although temporally scrambled and disjointed in its presentation, is of crucial symbolic importance. The "fabula," using the term in the Russian Formalist sense, contains an odd series of triangular configurations. Subsequent to her relation as a child with her father and dead mother, Joana becomes part of three other triangles: first, with her teacher and his wife; second, with her husband and his mistress; and third, with her lover and his former, spurned mistress. If we take as a model Freud's Oedipus, these triangles are abnormal in their function. Whereas the female version of the Freudian Oedipal triangle propels the girl into culture by establishing sexual difference and the acceptance of a passive femininity, here the many triangles insistently propel Joana out of the feminine position of passivity and subservience to men. These anoma'ous triangles result in Joana's breaking multiple bonds, ruptures that allow her to reassert, again and again, her artistic ambition.

As feminist criticism has seen, traditional narrative plots have curtailed female protagonists as severely as social scripts have limited women. To rescue Joana from a feminine fate that would deaden her artistic vocation, Lispector must rescue Joana from standard narrative plots, where a "happy ending" would render her subservient to a man. To use Rachel DuPlessis's term, Lispector must "disobey the novel" (DuPlessis 1985, 200). The very unconventionality of the plot events, as Joana flirts with, but escapes, marriage, adultery, and passionate love, has led critics to worry about the supposedly "unfinished" quality of the novel, and Joana to ponder, thinking of herself as a character of a narrative, "How can one end Joana's story?" (*WH* 159).

In her theory of the female spectator, Teresa de Lauretis examines the predicament of the female viewer of narrative cinema that is "the production of Oedipus" (de Lauretis 1984, 121), where the female is usually the passive object and the male, the active subject:

What manner of seduction operates in cinema to procure the consent, to engage the female subject's identification in the narrative movement, and so fulfill the cinematic contract? What manner of seduction operates in cinema to solicit the complicity of women spectators in a desire whose terms are those of Oedipus? (de Lauretis 1984, 137)

Lispector refuses for Joana the submission to a desire "whose terms are those of Oedipus," while acknowledging the lure of that desire. Lispector's use of triangular configurations encodes the "duplicity and ambivalence" (de Lauretis 1984, 156) that Teresa de Lauretis sees as a characteristic of female desire, a double desire that identifies simultaneously with passivity and action. At the same time the four triangles result in Joana's disentanglement from a passive femininity, thus challenging the constraint—for author, character, and reader—of Oedipal patterns in the production and reception of the text.

As a child Joana tells her father that she intends to be a hero when she grows up, and then follows a path marked by long and repeated struggles with accepted feminine roles. Lispector provides for Joana a cross-gendered lineage of a tender, nurturing father and a harsh mother, already dead. In the initial chapter, Joana, a little girl, plays by her father's side. Although the father works abstractedly at his typewriter, he does not represent a forbidding masculine "logos." He resists her interruptions, but can be persuaded to listen to the poems she composes, and he praises Joana's creative efforts.

Encouraging Joana, the father sees her as harboring a precious potential. He is maternal, and birdlike, as Hélène Cixous has seen (Cixous 1987b, 11), in his solicitous clucking over his little egg: "The child is left so much to her own devices, she's so thin and precocious. . . . He breathes rapidly, shaking his head. A tiny egg, that's it, a tiny, living egg. What will become of Joana?" (*WH* 15).

Joana's mother, who also escapes the usual gender demarcations, appears to Joana through the father's reminiscences:

She was called . . . he glanced at Joana—she was called Elza. She was refined, oblique, full of power. So quick and harsh in making judgements, so independent and embittered that from our very first meeting I accused her of being ruthless. (*WH* 25)

The father admires this unconventional woman and recognizes her superior intelligence. He wryly describes her presence in his family with metaphors of contagious illness and heterodox worship, in which the family appears as the feminine element subverted by the mother: "It was as if I had brought to its rosy and ample bosom . . . some contagious virus, a heretic, I don't know what . . . " (*WH* 26). In bed at night, the child is "afraid of Elza," a fear she tries to talk herself out of: "But you can't be afraid of your mother. A mother was like a father" (WH 26). However, the fear of the mother, not as an individual but as a role she herself might occupy, continues to haunt Joana's young life.

Joana will follow her father in her ambition to write, and her mother in her heresy against feminine orthodoxy. Unlike her mother, who, according to the father, "died as soon as she could" (*WH* 26), Joana will find not death but a stubborn victory. Against this background of parental figures, Joana establishes relations with others who will help or hinder (and be punished accordingly) her escape from the strictures of traditional femininity and her search for creative power. Joana's relations with the three men to whom she is erotically attached—her teacher, her husband, and her lover—act as a link to her literary ambition and feature a series of triangular configurations, in which "feminine" women, admired or debased, lurk in the background.

After the first peaceful triangle—the death of both parents precludes rivalry or struggle—comes the tense configuration of Joana, her teacher, and his wife. The teacher is a mentor who understands and encourages her unusual sensibility, but also exerts controlling pressure on her inner growth. She confides to him her innermost, inarticulate feelings: "Look, what I like most of all in the world . . . I feel it inside me, opening up . . . I could almost tell you what it is but I can't . . . " (*WH* 49). With his prodding, pointed questions and his demands for precision, the teacher validates her vague emotions and requires her to take the difficult step of putting them into words. Their connection—shot through with sexual longing—begins to border the murky realm of unwise attachments, where skewed, unequal power fosters what Lispector elsewhere calls *o amor ruim*, or controlling, self-serving "bad love." Joana's self-abasing adolescent infatuation encounters his desire, which he harshly terms "the selfishness and crude hunger of approaching old age" (*WH* 54). In the first of the two encounters with the teacher, Joana is overcome by jealousy of the teacher's wife, whose confident womanliness she contrasts with her own awkwardness and still shapeless body. This rival prods her into womanly growth and encourages her to detach herself from the teacher. Joana, sensitive to the cross-currents of sexual emotions in the triangle she forms with the teacher and his wife, feels obscurely that the friendship must end.

The second encounter with the teacher takes place much later, days before Joana's marriage. She needs to see him because "in a sense, she had the impresssion of betraying her entire past by marrying" (*WH* 104). The support she seeks, promised in the title of the chapter—"Under the Teacher's Protection"—turns out to be illusory. The teacher is now old, abandoned by his wife, suffering from heart disease: "The teacher was like a great castrated cat reigning in a cellar" (*WH* 105).[5] It is as if, in the teacher's illness and "castration," the plot, always favoring Joana, takes revenge for his earlier attempts to possess and shape her (albeit with her consent). Now Joana feels a kinship with the wife who left him: "that figure which she had so feared and detested, nearly always silent, the face aloof and imperious":

> In a moment of reminiscence Joana had discovered to her surprise that not only then but perhaps always, she had felt herself united to her, as if both of them had something secret and wicked in common. (*WH* 106)

The secret evil they share seems to be the rejection of a place that is subordinate to a powerful man. The wife, whom the teacher frequently betrayed, served as the suffering and menacing woman in the background during Joana's erotic attachment to him. They now simultaneously withdraw and humiliate him. Finding instead of the shelter she had hoped for a difficult interchange with a sick man whom she no longer captivates, Joana detaches herself from him with unspoken contempt: "She cruelly looked him straight in the eye. He repaid her with a look of mild indifference to begin with, and then almost immediately turned away, angry and disturbed" (*WH* 108).

Joana, her husband Otávio, and Lídia, her husband's current pregnant mistress and former fiancée, form another triangle through which Joana works out her conflicting attitudes toward loving and creating. Although she is the legitimate wife, Joana is also an interloper, for by marrying Otávio she undid his previous engagement to Lídia. The two women, each betraying and betrayed by the other, take part in a strange rivalry, in which Otávio is at once the prize and the victim. "I'm a feathered creature," Joana says, "and Lídia a furry one, and Otávio is lost between us, defenceless. How can he escape from my brilliance and promise of flight, or from the certainty of that woman?" (*WH* 133). This triangle defines sharply the lure and the danger in the roles of wife and mother, which Joana ultimately rejects, by providing another woman to live them out in her place.

Otávio admires and fears in Joana traits similar to those of her mother: "She speaks in such precise terms that it is terrifying, Otávio thought uneasily, suddenly feeling himself to be useless and effeminate. . . . There was a harsh, crystalline quality about her that attracted and repelled him at the same time" (*WH* 83). Mirroring the attitude of Joana's father toward her mother, Otávio recognizes Joana's brilliance with some misgivings. He, however, is the one who occupies comfortably the position of thinker. As a law professor, writing an article on public law and planning a book, he works at his desk and imagines himself performing before an approving audience: "As if everyone were standing by and nodding in approval: yes, that's right, very good" (*WH* 112). The tension between Otávio and Joana results not only from the love triangle but also from their intellectual competition. His intellectual identity seems to depend on Joana's quiescence: "I'm someone who works with my intellect, Joana is asleep in the bedroom" (*WH* 111-12).

The two scenes that center on Otávio as a thinker insist on his writing: one focuses on his consciousness as he writes, and the other on Joana's as she observes him reading and taking notes. This last scene opens the second part of the book, paralleling the initial chapter, in which Joana interrupted her father as he wrote. In this chapter, ironically entitled "The Marriage," Joana decides she will leave Otávio because marriage disturbs her solitude and depletes her inner life. As she sits idly by Otávio, reduced to fetching his books, she imagines a narrative in which she stands at the top of a staircase surveying an elegant gathering. A play of seeing and being seen, of high and low (with Joana and her surrogates occupying the high places), sets this narrative in motion, as it does most of the other examples of Joana's fictional imagination. She is unable to continue, despite the impression that the scene "kept on wishing to move on" (*WH* 97). Marriage has robbed her of her capacity to feel and think and to invent plots. She turns her anger against Otávio:

> He was the one who was feeling now, Joana thought. And suddenly, perhaps out of envy, without any thought, she hated him with such brute force that her hands were gripping the arms of the chair and her teeth were clenched. She panted for a few seconds, reinvigorated. . . . He was to blame, she thought coldly, looking out for a fresh wave of anger. . . . His presence and more than his presence: the knowledge that he existed robbed her of any freedom. Only on rare occasions now, in some fleeting escapade, was she able to feel. . . . He was robbing her of everything, everything. (*WH* 99-100)

The "feeling" Joana prizes is an active adventure, a probing, not a passive awareness of emotions. It is the force that drives her narration: "She herself, at the top of the stairs and with all her capacity for wanting to feel" (*WH* 102). Marriage is the awful wedge that splits her off from her powers. In the presence of Otávio, "her blood ran more slowly, its rhythm domesticated, like an animal that has trained itself to fit into a cage" (*WH* 100). Faced with the choice between love, even self-love, and following the creativity she obscurely desires, the latter seems more compelling: "Why go after him even if I love him? I don't like myself enough to like the things that I like. I love what I want more than I love myself" (*WH* 103).

Joana can feel and think, but it is the men, her father and Otávio, who write. The opening sentence of the novel refers to the father's writing: "Daddy's typewriter was tapping out tac-tac . . . tac-tac-tac . . . " (*WH* 11). On only two occasions, and then only briefly, does Joana write. In one of them, Otávio finds a sheet of paper inserted in a book by Spinoza with a few words in "Joana's wobbly handwriting. He couldn't resist looking closer: 'The beauty of the words: the abstract nature of God. Just like listening to Bach.' Why would he rather she hadn't written this sentence? Joana always caught him unawares. He felt embarrassed as if she were clearly lying and he were forced to deceive her by saying that he believed her" (*WH* 114-15). Joana's writing is, for Otávio, a transgression. Whether this is because she has done a poetic interpretation rather than an intellectual analysis of Spinoza's phrase, or because she has trespassed onto his territory by writing at all, she embarrasses him with what he considers to be "lies." Joana's verbal creations are mostly spoken, either to herself or to others: her ambition is "to speak," "to say." This scene is the only instance of Joana's acting as reader of a specific text, although she steals one book and borrows another from her teacher (anonymous books, in each case).

It is as props in Joana's acts of transgression that books appear most vividly. In a shoplifting incident, the stealing itself seems to matter above all else. Which book, or why Joana should want it, is never at issue. In another episode, more shocking in its cruelty, Joana shows her determination to avoid a nurturing role. She tells her husband she threw a book on purpose at an old man who had disgusted her by attempting to elicit her sympathy over a small bruise. The incident is dreamlike both in the vagueness of its circumstances and in the sharp details that depict the grotesque old man. In its telling, the episode itself functions as a weapon, which Joana hurls at her husband, to destroy similar expectations he might have of her. The grotesque old man stands for her husband, whom she habitually attacks with words or thoughts. As she sits and watches him work, her unspoken aggression almost reaches his consciousness: "What an animal, she thought. He interrupted what he was writing and looked at her in terror, as if she had thrown something at him" (*WH* 99).

We might read these two episodes in which books are used as props for her acts of transgression as emblematic of the need to insert the female word violently into a social circuit that neither expects nor desires it. Joana believes her husband "steals" her subjectivity; she herself must "steal" a place where she might display her language. Like the women writers who figured in Claudine Herrmann's metaphor as *voleuses de langue* (Herrmann 1980, 87), Joana, with no public space for her talent, must acquire it through theft. By throwing the book the woman writer unexpectedly purveys an unwanted, aggressive offering in place of the anticipated nurturance. Both acts encode the immoral freedom Joana associates with creation. Throwing the book, moreover, insists on the abrasive, cutting impact of her "text" upon the conventional expectations of the reader. It is worth noting that books function in symbolic exchanges and not, for Joana, as explicit objects of desire. In fact, although books would be the logical place for safekeeping Joana's precious moments of "saying" and "speaking," she rejects books as perhaps tainted with the encoded modes of creativity she wants to supersede.

A counterpoint to the battle waged by Joana and Otávio for words and power is the equally tense opposition between Joana and Lídia in their bid for Otávio. Lídia, tranquil in her passivity, attracts the longing and disdain that Joana directs at "the women who were merely female" (*WH* 21). Two surrogate mothers, Joana's aunt and the old cousin who brought up Lídia and Otávio (cousins themselves), represent a truly repugnant maternity. The fact that they are adoptive, not "real" mothers, disguises this harsh critique of stifling, narrow-minded, inappropriate motherhood. "The aunt's breasts could bury someone like a grave" (*WH* 34), Joana thinks. In contrast, Lídia stands for the good mother. Her procreativity represents a possible choice for Joana, an enticing refuge from the demands of her ambition. Lídia constellates in Joana powerful antithetical feelings of self-abasement and superiority. "It's enough to look at this woman to understand that no one could love me" (*WH* 132), Joana thinks. She compares her own luminous elusiveness to Lídia's solid maternal presence: "At her side no one slips and is lost for they can find support on her breasts—solemn, tranquil and pale, while mine are futile—or on her belly where there is even room for a child" (*WH* 133).

Joana's almost homoerotic attraction to Lídia also involves the desire to be the object of her maternal attentions and to subordinate herself to the comfort emanating from Lídia's adherence to a traditional role:

> I should like to spend at least a day watching Lídia go back and forth from the kitchen to the sitting-room, then have lunch with her in a quiet room—a few flies, the tinkling of cutlery—cool in the afternoon heat, wearing an old baggy robe in a floral pattern. Later in the afternoon, sitting beside her and looking on as she sewed, giving her a little assistance here and there, the scissors, the thread, waiting for bath-time and tea, it would be nice, spacious and refreshing. Was this perhaps what had always been missing in my life? Why is she so powerful? I suppose that because I have not had sewing afternoons, that this doesn't make me inferior to her. Or does it? It does, it doesn't, it does, it doesn't.
> (*WH* 136-37)

In a telling continuation, Joana imagines a motherly figure who will rescue her from her wayward path, unburdening her of her literary ambition:

> I know what I want: a woman who is ugly but wholesome with large breasts who will say to me: what is all this about inventing things? Enough acting up, come here at once!—A woman who will give me a warm bath, dress me in a white linen night-gown, braid my hair and put me to bed, thoroughly annoyed and muttering: Whatever next? You run around, eating at any old hour, you'll catch some illness if you're not careful, making up dramas, do you think that makes you important, drink up this bowl of hot broth. . . . You'll see how that face will soon fill out, forget all these foolish ideas and be a good girl. (*WH* 137)

As Joana steers her literary ambitions past the seductions of traditional feminine roles that would hinder or destroy them, she considers for a moment combining a self-directed life with reproduction. On a cruel impulse, she tells Lídia she will give up Otávio only if he first gives her a child. But the brief fantasy turns menacing: "My child will thrive on my strength and crush me with his life. He will distance himself from me and I will become his useless old mother" (*WH* 144).

If Lídia presents a model for behavior Joana finally rejects, another character, "the woman with the voice," offers a different means of connecting with the traditionally feminine woman. Seeing this woman as a sort of double for Lídia, Joana often speaks of the two in the same breath. Rather than arousing in Joana the fantasy of taking her place or becoming her child, "the woman with the voice" extends to her a call to narration. Joana is struck by a peculiar tone of voice she finds in an ordinary woman she meets when she inquires about a house for rent: "It haunted Joana throughout the entire afternoon. Her imagination pursued the woman's smile, her ample and tranquil body. She had no history, Joana discovered slowly" (*WH* 69).

Joana ascribes to this woman an unreflective, unimaginative self-coherence, emanating from a vital center that remains untouched by circumstances and events: "She was merely the life that flowed constantly inside her body" (*WH* 69). In Joana's imagined narrative of this woman's life—posited not as fiction, but as "discovery"—the woman undergoes brief moments of self-division, when she becomes, like Joana, "unhappy and intelligent." These subside, however, and an unreflexive existence reabsorbs her. About her (imagined) death, Joana affirms: "Her existence was so complete and so closely bound to truth that at the moment of surrendering and reaching her end, she probably thought, had she been in the habit of thinking: I never was" (*WH* 71). The woman's unthinking vitality paradoxically makes of her a "half-dead creature": . . . she understands life because she is not sufficiently intelligent not to understand it" (*WH* 71). In the novel's second and last instance of Joana's being moved to write, she registers her final appraisal of the woman, in a gesture motivated in part by revenge: "On a piece of paper [she] scribbled decisively in bold letters: 'The personality that does not know itself achieves greater fulfillment.' True or false? But in a sense she had taken her revenge by casting her cold, intelligent thought over that woman swollen with life" (*WH* 72). The character Joana creates—another example of the unquestioning woman whom, like Lídia, Joana both despises and envies—becomes a means for participating in and questioning attitudes she rejects. Self-divided, unhappy, intelligent, Joana scrutinizes her own disparate selves while imagining other selves that escape the punishment and prize of an analytic mind, an imaginative bent, and conflicting emotions.

In this episode, the metaphor "voice" points in two directions: to the woman's unthinking (or so Joana must imagine it) attunement to existence and to Joana's determination to put it into words. The woman lacks precisely the voice Joana has; Joana fears she may lack the greater authority of the woman's silent voice. Joana's narrative implies a sort of reciprocity, a continuum of mutual need between character and author. Yet, as always in Lispector, mutual need increases the undertones of aggression, the drive for separation and revenge. Writing, which requires participation and critical reflection, bonding and separation, allows for sympathy while also harboring the aggression so evident in Joana's beleaguered relations with both male and female figures.

A fourth and final triangle is made up of Joana, her lover, and a shadowy older woman in whose house the lover lives. The lover is another figure whose behavior miraculously conforms to Joana's need. She takes up with him — a man who follows her about in the street — soon after finding out about Otávio and Lídia's reunion. Unlike Otávio, who depletes her energies, the lover releases in her a flow of words by providing an eager, adoring audience. Joana is a fabulator, an inventor of narratives and poems that tell the "truth." For her to blossom, the lover adopts the self-negating role that she had assumed with Otávio. He is the one unable to speak and to "be": "One day, breaking the silence which he kept up when he was with Joana, he tried to speak: 'I have always been nothing' " (*WH* 155). Requiring his complete enthrallment to her talent, she presses him to see in her invented narratives representations of essential truths:

> "When I say these things . . . these crazy things, when I don't want to know about your past and I don't want to tell you about myself, when I invent words. . . . When I lie, do you feel I'm not lying?"
> "Yes, yes . . . " (*WH* 156)

Although they meet in his bedroom, their most thrilling interchange is not lovemaking, but narrating. As she speaks, inventing stories, poems, words (efforts somewhat more elaborate than her childhood compositions) brought forth in eager self-assurance, he is dazzled and pained by her luminous power:

> When she spoke, plenitude filled him like a great expanse and his anguish was that of the clear spaciousness above the water. Why did he feel astounded in her presence, awed as a white wall in the moonlight? He might perhaps suddenly wake up and call out: who is this woman? she is excessive in my life! (*WH* 157)

This literary exchange, in which Joana greedily nourishes herself with his faith and speaks while he listens, constitutes for Joana the height of love: "She had never loved him more than at such moments" (*WH* 157).

Meanwhile, in the background stands the third figure in the triangle, an older woman, "an affectionate and tiresome shadow" (*WH* 152) with whom Joana's lover lives. In Joana's mind, this woman's presence becomes, in some unexplained way, essential: "The presence of the other woman was so powerful in the house, that the three of them formed a couple" (*WH* 154). In contrast to the self-effacing, feminine woman, whose function is to suffer in the background, Joana appears as interloper, the one who "steals" what belongs to someone else. In her inappropriate black lace dress and painted face, this woman represents a spurned, pathetic sexuality:

> For one day [Joana] had caught a glimpse of her, the woman's broad shoulders concentrated into an indissoluble lump of anguish beneath her black lace dress. She had also watched her at other fleeting moments, passing from room to room, smiling quickly, escaping horribly. . . . The simpering, furtive, inviting glance of a whore, without glory. Her lips moist, chapped, large, smothered in lipsick. How she must love the man. Her fluffy hair was sparse and reddish from constant dyeing. (*WH* 154)

Described as an old prostitute presumably because she submits passively to mistreatment, the woman stands in diametric opposition to Joana, who adopts an active and dispassionate role with her lover in an exchange likened to a spiritual rape: "It was she who had violated that man's soul, who had filled it with a light whose evil he still hadn't fathomed. She herself had scarcely been touched" (*WH* 173). When Joana casts the woman in a motherly relation to her lover, she again entraps her in suffering, by imagining the woman tending to the room Joana and her lover share "like someone sewing her own son's shroud" (*WH* 155).

In this relationship, which is most supportive of Joana's verbal creativity, we also find in the background, as part of the "couple," the most debased of all the women in the novel. How can we interpret this disquieting threesome? The woman seems to perform a complex role, at once a reminder of the potential humiliation in the acceptance of a "housekeeping" position and a warning, by horrid example, against the possible lure of such passive subordination. Unlike Lídia's, her position is purely negative and repellent. This last triangle also seems to encode both the guilt and the triumph of a woman's pursuit of her artistic powers. As Adrienne Rich remarks, "For centuries women have felt their active creative impulses as a kind of demonic possession" (Rich 1979, 173). Joana's exercise of her talent here seems to bring about social havoc around her, by debasing the woman and entrapping the man in pathetic dependence. The lover suddenly and conveniently disappears, for reasons his long farewell note fails to explain. "They came to get me" (*WH* 172) is all he says, while protesting his abject devotion and intention to return. She suspects he has been arrested—but for what crime? In the dream logic of the plot, Joana has simply no further use for him, and his disappearance frees her from his clinging dependence. Like the teacher after she is through with him, a "great castrated cat," the lover also becomes a stricken cat: "She recalled the man's face during those last days, his eyes moist and bleary like those of a sick cat. And the skin around them, purplish and dark like a sun-set" (*WH* 172).

In the two final chapters of the novel, the plot provides for the departure of the men, husband and lover, from Joana's life. The fact that they literally "abandon" her thinly disguises her desire to be left alone. It is worth noting that Lispector's translation of the Joycean epigraph stresses the need for abandonment: "He was alone. He was unheeded" becomes, in Lispector's quotation, "He was alone. He was abandoned." About Otávio's departure, Joana thinks: "Why lie? She herself was the one who had left, and Otávio also knew it" (*WH* 173). She refuses the position he expects of her and that Lídia has already taken up. Bewildered by Joana's unconventionality, Otávio feels unmanned at her side: "He could not perceive her as a woman and his quality as a man became useless, and he was incapable of being anything other than a man" (*WH* 168). His departure is presented as a failure of courage; he refuses an adventure parallel to Joana's by refusing to live at her side.

Joana's voyage, with its unspecified destination, will symbolically bring her closer to her own wild heart. In this transposition of the romantic myth that casts the poet as hero, and his vocation as the object of his quest, Lispector assigns to Joana a double function: she is both quester and desired goal, for what she will "say" is hidden within herself. At the same time, Joana avoids, by leaving Otávio, the traditional feminine role of helper and mediator in a male hero's plot. As a child, she told her father she wanted to be a hero herself. Later, she asks, "How can one end Joana's story?" (*WH* 159) and thinks of herself as "my heroine" (*WH* 159). To be a hero, she must refuse ready-made social scripts that, for a woman, end in marriage. She tells Lídia that she has the strange impression that she never married, and that she always thought marriage would be the end: "After I marry nothing more can ever happen to me. . . . [T]o be a married woman, in other words, someone with her destiny traced out. From then onwards you simply have to wait for death" (*WH* 138).

For Joana, the devotion to her own artistic potential implies the refusal of socially constructed gender dichotomies. In the novel's closing paean to creativity, Joana seems to place herself beyond the deadly reach of gender roles. She both is and is not a woman:

> She was not a woman, she existed, and what was inside her were movements lifting her in constant transition. Perhaps at some time she might have altered with her savage strength the air around her and no one had noticed, perhaps she had invented without knowing a new substance with her breathing, she merely sensed what her small woman's head could never understand. (*WH* 178)

Her savage heart (*selvagem* in Portuguese means both "wild" and "savage"), its unknown terrain is coextensive with the natural world. The forces of her inner being are cast in terms of the elemental substances of air, water, fire, and earth (Sá 1979, 175-80) or animal vitality. The space she seeks for herself is as wide as all of nature, and untroubled by gender divisions that constrict women. In her verbal talent she will find a self-possession similar to the one she imagines for feminine women like Lídia. Metaphors of gestation, birth, and breath figure her creation and her art: "She would conclude once and for all the long gestation of childhood and from her painful immaturity her own being would burst forth, free at last!" (*WH* 185); "that miracle, the tender creature of light and air who was trying to live inside her" (*WH* 177).

Although Joana establishes connections between herself and the vast realms of nature, she breaks all bonds to other human beings. "She is vague and bold," Joana thinks about herself. "She doesn't love, no one loves her. . . . However, what's inside Joana is something stronger than the love one gives and what's inside her demands more than the love one receives" (*WH* 159). The novel posits loving and creating as inexorably incompatible. The need to squelch love in all its manifestations explains, perhaps, the peculiar aggression that informs the scenes in which Joana's verbal performances overpower an audience. One such scene establishes emphatically the connection between narration and aggression. Joana remembers that in boarding school she made up stories about the people around her, uncovering their hidden fatigue, sorrow, or despair "when she felt the need to test her power, to feel the admiration of her school-mates with whom she generally hardly spoke. Then she would coldly put on an act, inventing, resplendent as if wreaking vengeance" (*WH* 128). The effect on Joana's classmates was that of a humiliating constraint, of having to see through her eyes. "The more pliable ones murmured, already smiling, overcome: That's right, how do you know?"

> Little by little something disquieting, painful and awkward crept into that scene. They ended up laughing too much, nervous and dissatisfied. Joana, in high spirits, excelled herself, held the girls captive to her will and word, imbued with an ardent and cutting wit like the glancing strokes of a whip. Until, hemmed in at last, they breathed her brilliant and suffocating air. Suddenly feeling satisfied, Joana then stopped, her eyes dry, and her body shaking in triumph. Defenseless, sensing Joana's hasty departure and her contempt, the girls also withered away, as if ashamed. (*WH* 135)

In this scene, Joana's power to narrate and to "see" creates two victims: the subject of her fictions, whose suffering is exposed, and her listeners, who become dependent on Joana's will. In this grim narrative pact, the author's "victory" over her audience becomes exploitative. The display of her brilliance entails a heady traffic with evil. It is as if in order to break the grip of the social rule that obliges women to behave with kindness and nurturance, Joana had to wield the forces of a different order that narrative constellates. Narration for her is not an anodyne exchange but rather commerce with the forces of suffering and violence. Only those who are not afraid of these forces will dare "see" the truth. Her audience, although subjugated, yields uneasily to Joana's disquieting insights. Joana accepts her own ruthlessness along with the cruelty of the world, just as she did as a child, when she paid a visit to the chickens in her neighbor's backyard after enjoying roast chicken for dinner, maintaining with scrupulous vigilance her love for the birds both as friends and as food.

We find in this novel an unstable evaluation of the morality of writing, for Joana and, if we read her as representative, for the woman writer. Writing is aligned with stealing and lying, both by Joana (who alternates between Promethean pride and uncertainty about the validity of her efforts) and by Otávio, who expresses harsh disapproval. On the other hand, Joana associates writing, speaking, or saying with knowing, discovering, or seeing the "truth." By turns, she views her talent with self-abasement and self-aggrandizement, with the latter usually dominating. Violence and aggression define the transmission and reception of her "text"; at the same time, her inward meditations posit a harmony between creative impulses and the processes of nature.

Writing is for Joana, as it will continue to be for Lispector, an arena for the battle between warring forces within the subject, enacted in the text. The thinking and feeling that propel fictional invention are at odds with each other and gender marked. Joana, who claims both for herself, at times flings her "masculine" thought against the encroachment of "feminine" feeling, as in the episode of "the woman with the voice." At other times, feelings and sensations are pushed and pursued beyond the possibilities of logical comprehension. And "saying," with its links to emotions and the intellect, may set aside both these faculties in favor of senseless, sensuous signifiers:

> Then she invented what she must say. Her eyes closed, submissive, she uttered in a whisper words born at that moment, hitherto unheard, still fresh from creation—new and fragile buds. They were less than words, merely disconnected syllables, senseless, warm, flowing and criss-crossing, fertilized, reborn in a single being only to separate immediately, breathing, breathing . . . (*WH* 127)

Joana displays a deconstructive awareness of the capacity of language to escape intentionality. Thinking, feeling, and saying, not only are at odds, but also may be corrosive of one another:

> The distance that separates feelings from words . . . And the most curious thing of all is that the moment I try to speak, not only do I fail to express what I'm feeling, but what I'm feeling slowly transforms itself into what I'm saying. (*WH* 87)

> The worst thing of all is that she could cross out everything she had just thought. Once erected, her thoughts were like statues in the garden and she passed through, looking at them as she went on her way. (*WH* 18)

This novel explores, then, with exhilaration and persistence, the conflicting forces that make up subjectivity, shape intersubjective relations, and govern literary exchange. The triangular configurations that follow fast upon one another share in freeing Joana from the snares, even enticing ones, of female roles. This novel, with its withering critique of the damages the prevalent gender arrangements inflict on female talent, and its depiction of the aggressive lengths to which a woman must go to counteract their effects, was published in the same year Lispector entered a marriage to a fellow law school student that was to last some fifteen years. The life of proud solitude and undivided devotion to her art that Lispector chooses for Joana was not what she chose for herself. It is important to note this divergence in the paths of biography and fiction in a novel that has often been read autobiographically. In this novel, the first of Lispector's many texts that explore the conjunctions and disjunctions of writing and female gender, Joana's pursuit of her talent leads her to a deconstruction of gender dichotomies—but at a price. In a strictly gendered society, her only option is to embark on a solitary voyage that precludes loving and being loved. Lispector's young artist frees herself from social expectations and ethical constraints, but must go alone in search of her own wild heart.

II

In "The Misfortunes of Sofia" (*The Foreign Legion*, 1964), Clarice Lispector no longer envisions loving and writing as incompatible, forking paths for a woman. The nine-year-old protagonist's initiation into writing occurs as part of her intense love-hate attraction to a male teacher, coinciding with her beginning as a "woman." The tortuous harshness of love becomes a metaphor for the exigencies of the literary transaction.

The story borrows its title from a didactic novel for children by the Comtesse de Ségur (Sophie Rostopchine), which, in its translation from the French into Portuguese, became a staple of childhood reading in Brazil for many generations. In an upper-class setting in fin de siècle France, five-year-old Sofia succumbs to irresistible temptations, sampling a variety of small sins (greed, impatience, thoughtlessness, envy, jealousy, disobedience). Sofia, therefore, is not so much the name of Lispector's protagonist as an intertextual mask. Lispector's Sofia possesses her predecessor's waywardness and conviction of her own "badness," which the narrative frames as a kind of innocence. The position of the "I" in Lispector's story as subject and object of the narrative evokes autobiography,[6] as does the tone of intimate reminiscence and the theme of coming-into-writing of a young girl.

Although the girl is attracted to her teacher, there is no female rival in the background, no triangular configuration. Loving and writing are no longer parceled out to different women, but distill their parallel poisons simultaneously, in and through the heroine. This story, like others in *The Foreign Legion* and in *Family Ties* (1960), turns on an epiphanic moment, which a tense narrative dissects into contradictory movements. A narrative of crisis, of moments of extreme painful and joyful awareness, it relies on sentence-by-sentence work with paradoxes and antitheses. Lispector refers constantly to dichotomies (love-hate, innocence-sin, cowardice-courage) only to deconstruct them in order to show that both sides of the polarities are imbued with their opposites. This rhetorical strategy, with its vertiginous effect on the analytic mind, pushes the text beyond the reach of logic, probing what lies beyond rational thought, although not beyond the sinuous and insinuating power of words. Lispector alludes to this pressing toward the irrational and the unsayable in "Miraculous Fishing" (*The Foreign Legion*), one of her fragments about writing:

> To write, therefore, is the way of someone who uses words as bait: the word fishes for something which is not a word. When that non-word takes the bait, something has been written. Once the space between the lines has been fished, the word can be discarded with relief. But here the analogy ends: the non-word, upon taking the bait, has assimilated it. Salvation, then, is to read "absent-mindedly." (*FL* 119)[7]

Unlike the *dérèglements* of the surrealists, Lispector's subversions of logical thought use as instruments the processes of logic. With resignation, with suspicion, she partakes of and undercuts a contaminating reason: "In order to understand my non-intelligence, I was forced to become intelligent. (Intelligence is used in order to understand non-intelligence. Except that the instrument goes on being used—and we are unable to gather things with clean hands.)" (*FL* 118). Sofia's writerly initiation is fraught with contradictory, double-edged values of hyperbolic intensity. Writing is her treasure and also her disaster ("Os desastres de Sofia" is the Portuguese title). The interactions writing entails, also of unstable value, unsettle reader and author alike. The young girl, locked into habitually teasing and provoking the teacher she loves, perceives his stooped shoulders and ponderous manner as signs of a cowardly flight from another, more worthwhile practical or spiritual occupation. Her misbehavior manifests her childish "badness," and also her effort to "save that man": "I wanted what was good for him, and in return, he hated me. Bruised, I became his demon and tormentor, the symbol of the hell it must have been for him to teach that grinning, inattentive class" (*FL* 14). Sofia shifts back and forth from petulant child to seductress to self-abnegating savior, while the teacher shifts from being an authority she tests to becoming by turns an object of her "black dreams of love" (*FL* 14) and a weary, defeated man. The positions of "teacher" and "disciple" are subject to disconcerting reversals, as the girl and the man alternately occupy them. The danger to the teacher—what she seduces him into or saves him from—remains unspecified. Shifting, slippery metaphors figure the contradictory strains of their relationship. In a metatextual commentary, the narrator recognizes her only partial control over the repeated nets she casts to capture meanings:

> Without knowing that I was observing time-honoured traditions, yet with

that insight which the wicked are born with . . . I was playing the whore and he the saint. No, perhaps it was not that. Words anticipate and outstrip me, they seduce me and transform me, and if I am not careful it will be too late: things will be said without my saying them. (*FL* 14)

In the narrator's traffic with language, words, while teasing and seducing her toward the unknown, repeat the role the child plays with regard to the teacher.

The literary exchange at the center of this story begins when the teacher assigns to the class a paraphrase of a parable about a poor man who searches far and wide for the treasure he dreamed he would find. Returning home disappointed, he plants seeds in his own backyard and tends his garden so diligently that he thus comes by his wealth. The girl decides to alter the implicit moral of this "sad tale" extolling hard work:

Frivolously, I drew the opposite moral: something about a disguised treasure which exists where one least expects to find it, only waiting to be discovered. . . . I suppose that by willfully contradicting the real meaning of the story I somehow in writing promised myself that idleness rather than work would yield me many gratuitous rewards, the only rewards to which I aspired. . . . I would give everything I possessed for nothing, but I wanted everything in return for nothing. (*FL* 18-19)

The teacher's admiring reaction to her composition brings a truce to their war and disconcerts the girl with the loss of her enemy and support. If the teacher musingly discovers a treasure in his little enemy, the girl herself is made uneasy by the recognition of her unsuspected verbal powers.

Metaphors of orality, of incorporation and rejection by mouth, figure her troubled view of the literary exchange. She feels she has deceived him with "all that nonsense about the treasure" (*FL* 24). "He was like a beggar grateful for a plate of food, unaware that he had been given spoiled meat" (*FL* 24). It is she, however, who reacts to the teacher's praise with nausea, and runs outside at the end of the interview "with my hand over my mouth as if someone had broken my teeth" (*FL* 25). "That same night all this would be transformed into an irrepressible fit of vomiting that would keep all the lights on in my house" (*FL* 24). The mouth is the site both of vital, pleasurable incorporation and of repugnance, rejection, and possible poisoning; as such, it represents an author's ambivalent commerce with characters and readers, an exchange that includes sympathy and detachment, becoming the other or demeaning the other, proffering "truth" or inflicting lies.

Although the revelation of her talent has implications mainly for the girl herself, she projects her new awareness onto a grotesque vision of the teacher, in which what she sees reaches beyond the limits of what she understands. "Bristling, ready to throw up, although to this day I cannot know for certain what I saw. As if looking deep into someone's mouth, I suddenly saw the chasm of the world. What I saw was as anonymous as a belly open for an intestinal operation" (*FL* 22). She sees, on one level, the teacher's grotesque grimace as he attempts a smile of praise that resembles the inside of an eye, "an open eye with its quivering gelatine" (*FL* 23). These surrealist images of dismembered parts of the body evoke Dali, Magritte, or the eye sliced open in Buñuel's *Le chien andalou*. The organ of sight becomes implicated in the object it sees, undergoing itself the violence it witnesses. On another level, she confronts an overwhelming responsibility for seeing and accepting the wounds of the world and the bloody process of spiritual birth:

> Unable to understand, I knew I was being asked to accept him and his open belly; to receive his manly weight. . . . It was much too soon for me to see how life is born. Life being born is so much more bloody than dying. Dying is uninterrupted. But to see inert matter slowly trying to raise itself like a great living corpse—to see hope filled me with fear, to see life turned my stomach. (*FL* 23)

In the teacher's grotesque smile, the girl confronts nothing less than her "destiny": "reality was my destiny, and it was that part of me which hurt others" (*FL* 26). The call to see reality is equivalent to the acceptance of hurting and being hurt, a common denominator between writing and loving.

In the next to last paragraph of the story, her two vocations of loving and writing overlap so neatly that they become indistinguishable. The teacher's smile, prompted by his reading of her text, moves her like an annunciation: "Yes, just like an annunciated virgin. In allowing me to make him smile at last, the teacher had brought about this annunciation" (*FL* 27). But this revelation of her power over words links it to gender roles. She feels called upon to play "wife" in the battle of the sexes, a position that appears to be more powerful than its masculine counterpart. The gender distinctions blur, as the first person assumes the male guise of wolfman ("o lobo do homem," as in *homo homini lupus*, or the wolflike man or the wolf-in-man) and, simultaneously, of his victim; the "I" is then one of a pair of wolves:

> He [the teacher] had just transformed me into something more than the King of Creation: he had made me the wife of the King of Creation. For suddenly it fell to me, armed with claws and dreams as I was, to pluck the barbed arrow from his heart. Suddenly it became clear to me why I had been born with a harsh touch, why I had been born with no repugnance toward pain. What long nails you have! The better to scratch you to death and to pull out the fatal thorns, answers the wolf-man. What a cruel, hungry mouth you have! The better to bite you then blow on the wound so that I will not hurt you too much, my love, since I have to hurt you. I am the inevitable wolf, since life was given to me. What burning, clutching hands you have! So we may hold hands, which I need so much, so much,

so much!—the wolves howled, then looked nervously at their own claws before snuggling up to one another to make love and sleep. (*FL* 27)

The simple wickedness of the wolf in "Little Red Riding Hood" becomes a more complex, unavoidable, yet saving, violence inherent in the exchange of love and texts. In Lispector's intertextual reworking of this fairy tale, there is no ensnared innocent, only the dealings of wolves.

What, then, is the relation of gender to writing in this story of initiation? The text pits the discourse of reason and convention, voiced by the male teacher, who wants the class to paraphrase a moral tale, against the counterideological thrust of the girl's rewriting. She alters the teacher's moral, putting her trust in fortuitous discovery. Similarly, the girl's gropings, and the narrator's text, favor the alternate paths of irrational intuitions: "Was it towards the dark depths of ignorance that I seduced the teacher? And with the zeal of a cloistered nun" (*FL* 15). Later the narrator states: "Whatever I understood in the park was, with a shock of sweetness, understood by my ignorance" (*FL* 26). The male teacher is one of the many *professores* (Portuguese has no lexical distinction between "teacher" and "professor") in Lispector's fiction who represent an ambivalently admired and loathed authority of the rational intelligence, often already tottering or beleaguered. Although the teacher in this story is a sympathetic figure, he is duped, seduced, or "taught" by the arrogant little girl, who perverts the moral of his tale. The teacher, weary and defeated, his heavy body constrained in a too-small jacket, occupies the low-status position of elementary school teaching, in Brazil usually performed by women. The authority of his male discourse of reason and convention is, from the beginning, already undermined.

In the concluding words of the story, the significance of the girl's encounter with the teacher is framed as a double initiation: into writing and into the painful discordances of love.

> Thus it came about that in the large park surrounding my school, I slowly began to learn how to be loved, while enduring the sacrifice of not being worthy, if only to lessen the pain of one who does not love. No, that was only one of the reasons. The others make up different stories. In some, other claws, swollen with cruel love, have plucked the barbed arrow from my heart, and without repugnance for my pain. (*FL* 27)

In Portuguese, the same word, *história*, means "story," "history," and "lived events." To aspire to tell stories means the willingness to live stories, which for a woman in a gendered society requires confronting, although not necessarily conforming to, female roles. The narrator provides for the little girl a number of intertextual, metaphorical masks. Some are imbued with religious or biblical authority and suggest the channeling of sexual energies into a spiritual mission: prostitute who tempts a saint, ardent nun, annunciated virgin; others, like Sofia and the wolf, refer to secular texts about the transgressions of children. For Lispector, the ability to tell stories depends on the imaginative openness toward trying out, in their multifarious possibilities, and without fear of pain, the shifting positions for subject and object that the stories offer.

Whereas *Near to the Wild Heart* extricates the protagonist from the snares of femininity, sacrificing love in the process of avoiding feminine roles, "Sofia's Misfortunes" offers a more radical defense of the particular strengths of the female writer, by claiming that loving (when properly understood) and writing entail similar vulnerability and grasping assertiveness, a willingness to wound and be wounded, and to reject the Oedipal outcome of appropriate, passive womanhood. The violence required by this struggle shapes the subversive narrative structures and the antilogical, paradoxical linguistic texture of both of these stories of writerly initiation.

2
Female Power in *Family Ties*

In "The Daydreams of a Drunk Woman," the opening story of *Laços de família* (1960; *Family Ties*) the young protagonist arrives home completely drunk after an evening out with her husband. She feels her body grow enormously as surrounding objects turn into her own flesh:

> And, as she half closed her eyes, everything became flesh, the foot of the bed flesh, the window flesh, the suit her husband had thrown on the chair flesh, and everything almost hurt. And she became bigger and bigger, hesitant, swollen, gigantic. (*FT* 34)[1]

Many of the stories in the collection focus on such moments of physical or psychological aberration. The female protagonists are drawn into states of expanded perception in which they lose their "every-day soul, and how satisfying to lose it"(*FT* 31), and thus gain a power—exhilarating, threatening, and at times grotesque—normally inaccessible to them. But like the shrinking of swollen tissues, the power—or, more precisely, the illusion of power—recedes and dissipates, and the protagonists complacently take up again their normal, undistinguished lives.[2]

Family Ties contains Lispector's most celebrated, studied, and anthologized short stories, and yet the collection is rarely read in its entirety as a set of interacting texts. The more comprehensive perspective, although necessarily sacrificing the detailed reading that these stories invite and reward, allows us to discern patterns of interaction between gender and power in Lispector, an underlying theme of the collection and a persistent issue in all of her texts. These stories were written over a period of roughly a decade. Six of the thirteen stories had been published in another, little-noticed volume in 1952.[3] By 1955, at least four more of the *Family Ties* stories were completed, as were another four that Lispector would include in a later collection, *The Foreign Legion* (1964).[4] *Family Ties* is not, then, a compilation of all the short narratives Lispector had written to date, but a selection of complementary texts. As one critic observes, "The threads of a very well woven net organize themselves in each story, threads that join with those of other stories, composing a web of meanings that never cease to refer to one another"(Santos 1990, 8). In this chapter I argue that gender and power form one such nexus, and I attempt to trace its variations in the interplay of texts within the collection.

Psychoanalysis tells us that the family assigns and enforces gender. Lispector's scrutiny of gender roles entails a critique of the family, where she places her characters and their intimate crises. Three of the thirteen stories have male protagonists: in these, gender and power are also at issue and always problematic. The men, observed in different stages of life, from adolescence to old age, uneasily measure their supposed prerogatives and assess the price of conforming to masculine roles. The female protagonists, mostly middle-class women in an urban setting, also range from youth to old age. The stories in which they appear can be read as versions of a single developmental tale that describes patterns of female possibilities, vulnerability, and power in Lispector's world; the smaller number of stories with male protagonists offer a counterpoint. Lispector assigns traditional female roles to her characters: adolescents confronting the fantasy or reality of sex, mature women relating to men and children, and a great-grandmother presiding over her birthday party. Through the plots and the descriptions of her heroines' inner conflicts, Lispector challenges conventional roles, showing that the allegiances to others demanded by those roles exact their toll from the women who occupy them. The protagonists' moments of access to forgotten ambitions and desires produce dissatisfaction, rage, or even madness. The stories present the dark side of family ties, where bonds of affection hurt and constrict; yet the institution of the family sustains the characters, who might rebel, but usually do not escape its grip.

All the stories in Lispector's collection turn on an epiphany, a moment of crucial revelation (Sant'Anna 1973, 198) when, in the midst of trivial events, or in response to a chance encounter, her characters suddenly become conscious of repressed desires or unsuspected dimensions of their psyches. Whereas the men come to terms with the implications of a socially defined masculinity, the women experience the reverse of their accepted roles as mother, daughter, wife, as gentle, pardoning, giving females. In their moments of changed awareness, they may realize not only their imprisonment, but also their function as jailers of women and men. The epiphanies, mysterious and transgressive, bring to consciousness repressed material with potentially subversive power. The negative terms that often describe these moments—"crisis," "nausea," "hell," "murder," "anger," "crime"—convey the guilt and fear that accompany the questioning of conventional roles for both men and women characters (Santa'Anna 1973, 199). Interior monologues shaped by antithesis, paradox, and hyperbole display a wealth of opposing moral and emotional forces that resist logical definition. The convulsions of language in Lispector function in a way similar to the melodramatic gestures and rhetoric Peter Brooks has found in the works of Balzac and Henry James, resembling what he terms "the violence and extremism of emotional reaction and moral implication" in their prose:

> The more elusive the tenor of the metaphor becomes, the more difficult it becomes to put one's finger on the nature of the spiritual reality alluded to—the more highly charged is the vehicle, the more strained with pressure to suggest a meaning beyond. . . . To the uncertainty of the tenor, corresponds the heightening of the vehicle. (Brooks 1985, 11)

In Lispector, the hyperactivity of language in moments of crisis dramatizes the force fields that move her characters' consciousness, without ever simplifying their dilemmas into unambiguously rational terms. After these crises, when the recognition of their restrictions gives the protagonists a glimpse of greater freedom, many pull back, returning to a confinement they cannot or will not change. The intensity of their conflicts may be enlightening for the reader, but the characters return to their previous situations, which they have questioned for only a moment.

Two of the three tales of adolescent initiation in *Family Ties* have women protagonists. In "The Beginnings of a Fortune," a young boy suddenly fascinated with money grasps its connection with power and its usefulness in attracting girls. Yet he also sees that possession of "a fortune" would entail vulnerability to the greed of others. By the end of the story, he is, nevertheless, eager to continue acquiring money and financial information. The plots of the two stories with female protagonists, "Preciousness" and "Mystery in São Cristóvão" (see chapter 5 for further discussion), are parallel on a symbolic level: both hinge on the intrusion by several young men into a young woman's private domain. In "Preciousness," an adolescent undergoes a violent sexual "initiation" when two young men, passing strangers, reach out and briefly touch her body. After the first shock, she accepts and turns to advantage this negative experience, darkly intuiting it as a lesson about her fragile individuality in a world of powerful men. "Mystery in São Cristóvão" reworks in parable form a similar version of female sexual initiation. Three young men trespass into "the forbidden ground of the garden" (*FT* 135) to steal hyacinths as a young girl watches from her window. The four participants share a mute epiphany; then, as the girl screams, the young men guiltily slip away, leaving behind a "hyacinth—still alive but with its stalk broken" (*FT* 138).

The male and female initiation tales offer, then, a number of contrasts: activity versus passivity; a young boy who seeks wealth and power versus young girls who are "precious" themselves, metaphorically identified with jewels and flowers; preoccupation with acquisition versus concern with self-protection; entrance into the world of economic and social exchange versus fearful retreat into oneself. Development, for the young girls, clearly will not proceed according to the male model.

It is in a context of attachment to and affiliation with others that the women characters develop. After being initiated into the vulnerability to which their female sexuality exposes them, they find protection and a measure of satisfaction in family ties. We see in other stories several of Lispector's women safely ensconced in a domestic life. The stories reflect the matrifocal organization of Brazilian society, where the extended family still prevails, so much so that the word *família usually refers not only to the small nuclear family, but also to a numerous network of relatives. The title story shows most clearly the ambivalent function of the family in the whole collection. In "Family Ties," the power a woman wields within the family has a negative, constricting side: deprived of the chance to develop herself beyond the scope of the family, she attempts to control those close to her.*

"Family Ties" opens as Catherine says good-bye to her elderly mother at the train station, feeling an awkward tenderness and relief. With this scene between the two women, as well as with flashbacks and the narration of the emotional consequences of the mother's visit, the story touches on several types of family relationships: mother/daughter, mother-in-law/son-in-law, grandmother/grandson, husband/wife, and mother/son, all presented as subtle or not-so-subtle struggles for power. As Catherine looks at her mother through the train window, she becomes aware of the strong, but ambivalent, bonds they share:

> "No one else can love you except me," thought the woman, smiling with her eyes, and the weight of this responsibility put the taste of blood in her mouth. As if "mother and daughter" meant life and repugnance. (*FT* 117)

Relieved of her mother's company, the daughter recovered her "steady manner of walking—alone, it was much easier" (*FT* 119). However, that tie to her mother also facilitates an emotional availability: "She seemed ready to take advantage of the largesse of the whole world—a path her mother had opened and that was burning in her breast" (*FT* 120). This very openness to others leads Catherine, it seems, to attempt to bind her son to her in the same way she was bound to her mother. The last third of the story is told from her husband's point of view. Excluded and jealous, he watches Catherine and their small son from a window, perceiving their intense interaction:

> At what moment is it that a mother, hugging her child, gives him this

prison of love that would descend forever upon the future man. Later, her child, already a man, alone, would stand before this same window, drumming his fingers on the windowpane: imprisoned.... Who would ever know at what moment the mother transferred her inheritance to her child. And with what dark pleasure. (*FT* 122)

Here, the metaphorical prison entraps all members of the family: the father, who also speaks about his own predicament, sees the male as victim of the imprisoned and imprisoning female, the mother, who transmits this family tie to the next generation. The male power, deriving from his role in the world outside the home, does not prevail in the domestic world of intimate relationships, where his wife has a power at least equal to his own:

He knew that if his wife took advantage of his situation as a young husband with a promising future, she also looked down on the situation, with those sly eyes, running off with her thin, nervous child. The man became uneasy. Because he could only go on giving her more success. And because he knew that she would help him to achieve it and would hate whatever they achieved. (*FT* 122)

Despite their dissatisfactions, it seems clear that at least the husband wishes to preserve the status quo. " 'After dinner we'll go to the movies,' the man decided. Because after the movies it would be night at last, and this day would break up like the waves on the rocks of Arpoador" (*FT* 124). For the husband, the events of the day appear as minor, if recurrent, crises within the sustaining institution of the family.

The family as context for female development in Lispector's stories is, then, both positive and negative. Although it affords women the satisfaction of affirming ties to others, it also confines them to the subordinate role of ministering to others' needs and deprives them of an active agency in pursuing their private desires. The narrator of "Love" measures the rewards of a domestic life for the protagonist Anna, and hints at her sacrifices:

Through indirect paths, she had happened upon a woman's destiny, with the surprise of fitting into it as if she had invented that destiny herself. The man whom she had married was a real man, the children she mothered were real children. Her previous youth now seemed strange, like an illness of life. She had gradually emerged to discover that one could also live without happiness: by abolishing it she had found a legion of persons, previously invisible to her, who lived their lives as if they were working— with persistence, continuity, and cheerfulness. (*FT* 38)

Several protagonists face their crises from a similar perspective. Women devoted to love, marriage, and children discover within themselves allegiances that subvert those roles. These stories follow the generic model that Susan J.

Rosowski proposes in her article "The Novel of Awakening." Lispector's characters also attempt to find value "in a world that expects a woman to define herself by love, marriage, and motherhood" (Rosowski 1983, 68). For each protagonist, "an inner imaginative sense of personal value conflicts with her public role: an awakening occurs when she confronts the disparity between her two lives" (Rosowski 1983, 68). Lispector's protagonists also follow Rosowski's model in awakening to conflict and limitations. Their social world and their own conforming social selves cannot accommodate new allegiances. They discover that their loyalty to others has excluded possibilities for themselves. As Lispector puts it in a story from another collection, "To be loyal is not a clean thing. To be loyal is to be disloyal to everything else" (*FL*, 53). Four stories from *Family Ties* —"Love," "The Imitation of the Rose," "The Buffalo," and "Happy Birthday"—are Lispector's versions of this kind of awakening.

In "Love," Anna's everyday awareness of herself in her thriving domesticity is figured in images of prospering plants: "Like a farmer. She had planted the seeds she held in her hand, no others, but only those. And they were growing into trees" (*FT* 38). Although "at a certain hour of the afternoon the trees she had planted laughed at her" (*FT* 38), Anna feels steady in her chosen course until a casual encounter upsets her equilibrium. From a tram, she sees a blind man standing on the street, calmly chewing gum. His mechanical, indifferent acceptance of his fate perhaps mirrors for Anna her own blindness and restriction. The blind man is also a victim of the brutality of nature, which maims some of its creatures, a threat Anna usually forgets. When Anna continues her meditation in the botanical garden—a place that confines natural growth, forcing it to follow a prearranged plan—a nausea analogous to Sartre's *nausée* overtakes her: "a vague feeling of revulsion which the approach of truth provoked" (*FT* 44). The initial tranquility she perceives in this enclosed garden gives way to a disquieting vision of a secret activity taking place in the plants, as decay encroaches upon ripeness:

> On the trees the fruits were black and sweet as honey. On the ground there lay dry fruit stones full of circumvolutions like small rotted cerebrums. The bench was stained purple with sap. . . . The rawness of the world was peaceful. The murder was deep. And death was not what one had imagined. (*FT* 43)

The lesson she learns in the garden unsettles Anna's sureness about her immanent family world, about the seeds she planted that are growing into trees. At home, guilt-ridden for her transgressive thoughts, Anna feels both threatened and dangerous: "The slightest movement on her part and she would trample one of her children" (*FT* 47). In her final ruminations on the afternoon, Anna sees the blind man, "hanging among the fruits in the botanical garden" (*FT* 47). The blind man, as Anna's double, provides a frightening vision of her own destiny: death among the rotting fruit as a consequence of her stunted capacity for transcendence and lack of personal freedom in the life she has chosen. Yet, after a reassuringly ordinary evening at home, Anna seems content to forget her disturbing afternoon: "As if she were snuffing out a candle, she blew out the day's small flame" (*FT* 48), the light of her confused enlightenment, which could threaten her domestic life if it were allowed to burn.

"The Imitation of the Rose" contains a similar configuration of opposing forces: a familiar, domestic world threatened and undermined by the laws of another realm. For Laura, who has just returned from a mental hospital, images of light represent her powerful attraction to madness, suggesting that in madness she finds insights otherwise unavailable to her. Laura's dutiful relief at being "well" again, her drab descriptions of herself and her activities, contrast with her luminous, lively account of her mad self. Sleepiness, fatigue, obsession with method, cleanliness, and detail, a certain slowness of body and mind that bores others as well as herself—all these signal that Laura is "well." An alert wakefulness, clarity of mind, a sense of independence, of possessing extraordinary powers, accompany her returning madness.

In the encounter that sets off the struggle between sanity and madness, Laura admires the wild roses in her living room. The conflict between the impulse to send the roses to a friend and the desire to keep them for herself reflects Laura's lifelong struggle between accommodation to the wishes of others and assertion of her own subjectivity. She can only satisfy herself and what she perceives as society's demands by an exaggerated rendition of the role of a giving, submissive woman. The roses, in their beauty, exemplify a distinct, glorious self-sufficiency that Laura denies herself: "Something nice was either for giving or receiving, not only for possessing. And, above all, never for one to *be*. . . . A lovely thing lacked the gesture of giving" (*FT* 66). Yet as soon as Laura decides to give away the roses, her madness begins to return: "With parched lips she tried for an instant to imitate the roses inside herself. It was not even difficult" (*FT* 68-69). Tranquillity, self-sufficiency, and clarity signal Laura's changed state; she sits "with the serenity of the firefly that has its light" (*FT* 71). The story ends with the husband's view of Laura, whom he watches with a fear and respect that only her madness can elicit: "From the open door he saw his wife sitting upright on the couch, once more alert and tranquil as if on a train. A train that had already departed" (*FT* 72). This final image implies that only in madness can Laura assert her independence from the desires of others. She departs in the metaphorical train of madness, since other departures are beyond her capacity.

The role of woman in love limits severely the protagonist of "The Buffalo," who only senses her deficiencies when her husband or lover abandons her, depriving her of support. Feeling mutilated and incomplete, she visits a zoo in a conscious search:

But where, where could she find the animal that might teach her to have her own hatred? That hatred which belonged to her by right but which she could not attain in grief? . . . To imagine that perhaps she would never experience the hatred her forgiving had always been made of. (*FT* 152-53)

She senses that she is the one who is caged, "a female in captivity" (*FT* 153), while a free animal watches her from the other side. A visual confrontation with the buffalo—similar to Anna's with the blind man and Laura's with the roses, except that the buffalo returns her stare—allows her access to a wide and dangerous world, where she might free herself from her own compulsion to love and pardon. She looks to the buffalo, with its narrow haunches and hard muscles, as a masculine presence, the embodiment of her hatred and her strength "still imprisoned behind bars" (*FT* 155-56). She becomes terrified by the hatred that she projects onto the animal and that he in turn releases in her. As their encounter continues, it is couched in terms of a deadly struggle:

Innocent, curious, entering deeper and deeper into those eyes that stared at her slowly, . . . without wanting or being able to escape, she was caught in a mutual murder. Caught as if her hand were stuck forever to the dagger she herself had thrust. (*FT* 156)

Perhaps not ready to allow herself to hate, the woman faints in the final scene: "Before her body thudded gently on the ground, the woman saw the whole sky and a buffalo" (*FT* 156). Fainting signals, no doubt, her failure of nerve: a traditionally feminine strategy of withdrawal, it obliterates from consciousness her involvement and insights. Yet the image of the open spaces of the sky, ambiguous as it is becomes in conjunction with the fainting, seems to offer, in a story cluttered with cages, the possibility of release.

The moments of insight mostly visited upon young and middle-aged protagonists are, in "Happy Birthday," briefly available to an old woman celebrating her eighty-ninth birthday. She belatedly rejects her family, implicitly questioning her own role as a prototypical matriarch. Her power and the bonds of love have already been eroded, and her family gathers to mimic the appearance of closeness. The narrative method—a mosaic of interior monologues interspersed with dialogues and the narrator's remote, at times ironic, commentary—shows the resentment and hostility between members of the family and presents the protagonist as others see her as well as how she sees herself. In a Kafkaesque progression reminiscent of "The Judgment," the old woman at first appears decrepit and later demonstrates a surprising, malevolent vigor.

As the story opens, she is propped up, ready for the party: "There she was, stationed at the head of the table—an imposing old woman, large, gaunt, and dark. She looked hollow" (*FT* 75). She remains aloof and passive until urged to cut the cake: "And unexpectedly, the old lady grabbed the knife. And without hesitation, as if by hesitating for a second she might fall on her face, she dealt the first stroke with the grip of a murderess" (*FT* 78). Cutting the cake rouses the old woman from passivity; she goes on to shatter her image as dignified and respected mother. The metaphorical association of cutting/killing continues, linking the birthday gestures with those of a funeral: "The first cut having been made, as if the first shovel of earth had been thrown . . ." (*FT* 78). As the matriarch surveys her family "with her old woman's rage" (*FT* 80), Lispector resorts again to the recurring images of female imprisonment and powerlessness:

> She was the mother of them all. And, as her collar was choking her, she was the mother of them all, and powerless in her chair, she despised them. She looked at them, blinking. . . . How could she, who had been so strong, have given birth to those drab creatures with their limp arms and anxious faces? . . . The tree had been good. Yet it had rendered those bitter and unhappy fruits. (*FT* 79-80)

As her scorn and anger mount, the old woman curses, spits on the floor, and demands a glass of wine. The imagery and elements of the plot, with their origins in primitive and contemporary ritual—birthday party, funeral, spitting, cursing, wine—assimilate the old woman's revolt into the very institutions she challenges, suggesting that her anger and its ritualistic expression can be encompassed within their framework.

The old woman rails against her loss of power; in a sense she is a victim of old age. Her dominance stemmed from her personal capacity to play the most powerful role traditional Brazilian society allowed women: that of mother in a mother-dominated extended family. Her ability to command attention is eerily revived when she cuts the cake, spits, and curses. These actions serve as a crude demonstration of the willfulness that, in her prime, she would have manifested in more subtle and socially sanctioned ways. Yet this old woman, like Lispector's other protagonists, is also ultimately a victim of her social role. Her power issued from a control of others that is neither healthy nor enduring. One of her sons, observing that "she had not forgotten that same steady and direct gaze with which she had always looked at her . . . children, forcing them to look away," thinks that "a mother's love was difficult to bear" (*FT* 85). Because she cannot rule their lives she despises her children. By showing the lovelessness and will to power of this mother's love, Lispector suggests that the role of matriarch affords a false power that entraps women as well as their families.

After the old woman's outburst, the narrative method returns to external presentation. She relapses into an enigmatic passivity, clutching the ghost of her power: "Seated at the head of that messy table, with one hand clenched on the tablecloth as if holding a scepter, and with that silence which was her final word. . ." (*FT* 83). Like so many of Lispector's female protagonists, after a brief influx of power, she returns finally to her initial situation. As they move from youth to old age, the protagonists of *Family Ties* also trace a circular path, beginning and ending in passivity—from the withdrawal of a frightened young girl to the abstraction of an old woman whose power over her family, repressive in itself, is spent.

Through the plots and interior monologues of her characters, Lispector questions, as we have seen, the conventional roles she assigns to her protagonists. The tendency to subvert stereotypes in characters and plot recurs on the level of language. Lispector destroys and recreates the meanings of certain ordinary words, redefining them through paradoxical formulations. In "Love," the title word acquires multiple and contradictory meanings as the protagonist attempts to align her confused yearnings with the *eros* and *caritas* she had always believed gave direction to her life. In "The Imitation of the Rose," madness takes on a positive value, signifying the expansion of Laura's independence and self-esteem—at the end of the story Laura is "serene and in full bloom" (*FT* 71)—without, of course, losing its acceptation of illness, the delusion of power. Anger in "The Buffalo" becomes the elusive object of a quest, whereas pardon is defined as covert hatred. A reversal of values also occurs in the imagery: the thriving plants, metaphorical analogues of Anna's domesticity, reappear on the literal level as the lush and rotting vegetation in the botanical garden; the birthday party is described in terms of a funeral; family ties appear as chains and cages. The tendency to redefine words and concepts, to reverse traditional metaphorical associations or to draw images from negative and antithetical realms supports and furthers Lispector's questioning of "a woman's destiny."

Lispector's protagonists, as they shift from one set of specific circumstances to another, repeatedly find themselves entrapped by their eager compliance with confining social roles. Their potential development—the ability to move toward the greater autonomy they desire in their moments of insight—again and again falters and stops short. For the youngest protagonists, the prison is their own fearful passivity in a society that accepts as normal the intrusions by men such as the ones they experience. Anna's attachment to domestic routines blocks her from participating in a wider social and moral world, which both frightens and exhilarates her, and whose outlines she only obscurely intuits. For Laura, living according to others' expectations and suppressing her own desires leads to madness, an illusory escape into another prison. The woman in "The Buffalo" is caged by her inability to recover emotions she had long repressed, and in "Happy Birthday" and "Family Ties," mother-love itself imprisons. These women start out and remain in spiritual isolation. Locked in desired, yet limiting, relationships with husbands and children, they find no allies in other women— mothers, friends, or daughters—who if they appear at all are rivals and antagonists. Once the expansive insights of their epiphanic moments fade away, their only power lies in passing on an imprisoning motherly love to their children.

Two stories with adult male protagonists offer variants of the gender-linked crises of the women by probing the requirements of the masculine role. In "The

Crime of the Mathematics Teacher," the nameless protagonist, another of Lispector's *professores*, is defined by the clear thinking his profession demands: "There was no confusion in the man's mind. He understood himself with cold deliberation and without any loose threads" (*FT* 141). The narrator, however, makes much of his nearsightedness, of his putting on and removing his glasses, as if to imply that his lucidity is an obstacle to insight, just as the confusion of the female characters is a mode of understanding. The teacher attempts to expiate the crime of abandoning a dog whose love he was unable to reciprocate, and whose vulnerability tempted him to use it cruelly. "Each day you became a dog that could be abandoned," he thinks, addressing the absent dog. "One could choose. But you, trustfully, wagged your tail" (*FT* 144). With questionable symmetry, the teacher atones for the abandonment by burying a substitute, a dead stray dog, in a private ritual. We now see, from the point of view of the perpetrator, the "crime" of betrayal, also committed by the man who abandoned the protagonist of "The Buffalo": His "great unpunishable crime was not loving her" (*FT* 156). The mathematics teacher reassures himself that "no one goes to hell for abandoning a dog that trusted in a man. For I knew that this crime was not punishable" (*FT* 145).

In this story, the problem of being a man shades into the problem of being righteously human: because the teacher abuses his power he betrays his manhood. If, as one critic suggests, the dog symbolically represents a human partner in a love relationship (Santos 1986, 41), the teacher confronts from another perspective and with different results the issue that also troubles the women characters: how much caring does one owe to others and how much to oneself? The man discovers that his crime—"the debt that, disturbingly, no one required him to pay" (*FT* 146)—is unpunishable, not only by society but also by himself. He compounds his initial betrayal with a further one. "And now, even more mathematical, he sought a way to eliminate that self-inflicted punishment" (*FT* 146). He digs up the unknown dog, "[renewing] his crime forever. . . . And, as if that were still not enough, he began to descend the slopes, heading toward the intimacy of his family" (*FT* 146). Being a man, in this story, necessarily entails not being enough of a man, with its requirements of living up to strict standards of virtue. Being a man, however, also assures him of a power that not even his victim would question: "Powerful as I am, I need only choose to call you. Abandoned in the streets you would come leaping to lick my face with contentment and forgiveness" (*FT* 146). The man's ritual, with its lucid but empty gestures that offer an illusion of symmetry and mathematical rigor, but in no way aid the victim of his crime, serves ultimately to reassert his right to infringe unchallenged the moral rules he himself would wish to uphold.

"The Dinner," a story seldom discussed by critics,[5] also addresses the prerogatives and challenges of manhood. It is the only first-person narrative in *Family Ties* and, as such, presents a subject actually shaping a narrative, without a narrator's mediation. In a restaurant, a younger man watches with fascination and repulsion (emotions that converge readily in Lispector's fiction) a seemingly powerful old man who gulps down his red wine and red meat while fighting back tears. The plot consists exclusively of the young man's minute observations, supplemented by his own conjectures, of the grotesquely amplified movements of the old man, who eats his dinner and then leaves the restaurant.

Participating in a chain of voyeuristic acts, the reader witnesses the narrator's observation and private thoughts about the old man, who struggles with himself as he consumes his food, unaware of the sharp eyes that watch him. He resolutely takes nourishment, refusing to give way to a major grief, or so the narrator imagines, as he sees him falter and recover or wipe away tears. The young man sees him "as one of those elderly gentlemen who still command attention and power" (*FT* 99), "still enormous and still capable of stabbing any one of us" (*FT* 101), "the old child-eater." The strength of the patriarch derives from his single-minded use of others to increase his own power, a pursuit authorized by traditional gender roles and displayed in his greedy attack on the meat and wine. His command extends to his control of his emotions, in a spectacle that fascinates his observer. The narrator's reactions resemble those of the women characters in their epiphanic moments: "[The old man] expresses with gestures the most he can, but I, alas, I fail to understand . . . I feel gripped by the heaving ecstasy of nausea. Everything seems to loom large and dangerous" (*FT* 99-100). The narrator understands without understanding, as he witnesses a ruthless male power on the brink of collapse, the dark side of traditional masculinity, which in turn threatens his own sense of himself. "But I am still a man," he reassures himself in the final paragraph of the story, as he attempts to salvage his manhood from the spectacle he has just observed:

> When I have been betrayed or slaughtered, when someone has gone away forever, or I have lost the best of what I had left, or when I have learned that I am about to die—I do not eat. I have not yet attained this power, this edifice, this ruin. I push away my plate. I reject the meat and its blood. (*FT* 101)

The power he has not yet attained, part and parcel of the role of "old patriarch," is a power he may not want, having witnessed—or imagined—the violence it requires.

Although in *Family Ties* Lispector focuses on the constraints of women caught in traditional roles, her dissection of gender does not result in simple feminist fables of powerless women preyed upon by ruthless men. The oppression is more subtle and far-reaching for both the men and the women who confront its impersonal injunctions. The Brazilian writer Rubem Braga comments, in a letter of March 4, 1957, in response to nine of Lispector's stories (judging by the date, several of the *Family Ties* stories would have been among them): "It's funny how you touch and enrich me at the same time that you hurt me a little, making me feel less solid and secure" (Clarice Lispector Archive). At least part of this discomfiture results, I would suggest, from Lispector's challenges to the fixities of gender roles.

In most of the stories, an unobtrusive narrator provides the gaze that frames the characters. Their struggles are observed with an ambivalent, ironic eye that alternately exalts and puts them down, oscillating between sympathy and disdain. These oscillations are particularly marked in the stories that transpose to a parodic register Lispector's scrutiny of female power. In "A Chicken," a story that repeats the plot of failed escape from the confining roles of nurturing and submission, the limitations of the female role take on the sharpness of caricature. The protagonist, a chicken about to be killed for Sunday dinner, escapes her fate by setting off on a mad flight across the rooftops. Pursued and brought back by the man of the house, the flustered chicken lays an egg. The little girl who witnesses this surprising outcome persuades her mother to spare the chicken's life and adopts her as a pet. She seems to intuit a similarity between the chicken's predicament and the possibilities her own future may hold.

Another girl has the same understanding of chickens in a story from a different collection, which begins: "Once upon a time there was a little girl who observed chickens so closely that she knew their soul and their intimate desires" (Lispector 1971, 140). Gender determines the meaning of the chicken's adventure. During her escape the chicken is described as "stupid, timid, and free. Not victorious as a cock would be in flight" (*FT* 50). In her attempt to cast off the passivity expected of her and to assert her independence, the chicken echoes the central action of several other stories. Acquiring a "family tie" ends the chicken's adventure. It literally saves her life, but it does not provide her with enduring dignity or even safety. Her reprieve lasts many years, but not forever: "Until one day they killed her and ate her, and the years rolled on" (*FT* 52). Like the women she represents, the chicken's dilemma takes the form of an opposition between independence and nurturing: women may choose one role but not both, and Lispector's women end up settling for the nurturing role. Occasionally she recalls her "great escape":

> Once in a while, but ever more infrequently, she again remembered how she had stood out against the sky on the roof edge ready to cry out. At such moments, she filled her lungs with the stuffy air of the kitchen and, had females been given the power to crow, she would not have crowed but would have felt much happier. (*FT* 52)

Ellen Moers comments on women authors' use of birds "to stand in, metaphorically, for their own sex" (Moers 1976, 245). The chicken in this and later stories is Lispector's comically distorted image of the selfless, nurturing female incapable of sustained self-determination. The perspective implicit in this choice of metaphor, and in the abrupt shifts in tone from sentimentality to a blunt deflation, includes compassion, but also condescension, an attitude that carries over to Lispector's presentation of women in other stories of *Family Ties*. Most of the stories end with the female protagonists silent and described from an external vantage point, perhaps another sign of the author's desire to distance herself from her characters. In contrast to Lispector's first novel, where Joana boldly disdains the constrictions of feminine roles, in these short stories Lispector shows in excruciating detail protagonists bound in "women's destinies" and measures the extent of their disadvantage. It is tempting to suppose that these stories may have functioned for her as a kind of exorcism. Through this repeated exercise, Lispector could perhaps free herself—and her future women characters—for richer, more varied roles. Indeed, Lispector's imagination seems to require repeated incursions into the same themes. As one of her narrators states, "How many times will I have to live the same things in different situations?" (quoted in Hill 1976, 141). Lispector allows her later female protagonists greater independence and engages them in spiritual quests that are not invariably cut short by a return to confining domesticity.

The predominantly bleak view of female possibilities in *Family Ties* contains a curious exception, represented by the grotesque, almost fantastic protagonist of "The Smallest Woman in the World." This story elaborates on a supposedly documentary anecdote: a bewildered explorer meets the smallest member of the smallest tribe of African pygmies—a tiny pregnant woman, measuring a foot and a half—and names her Little Flower. Readers of the Sunday newspaper react to her story and see her life-size picture. With disconcerting shifts in tone, the little woman is alternately presented as subhuman ("as black as a monkey" [*FT* 89]; "she looked just like a dog" [*FT* 90]); and exquisitely suprahuman ("For surely no emerald is so rare. The teachings of the wise men of India are not so rare. The richest man in the world has never set eyes on such strange grace" [*FT* 90]).[6] Little Flower herself, oblivious both to her debasement and her exaltation, experiences an epiphany and also sparks moments of insight in other characters. Women of all ages seem fascinated by this hyperbolic representative of the fragility and powerlessness associated with their sex. One woman fights against an involuntary identification with Little Flower: "Looking into the bathroom mirror, the mother smiled, intentionally refined and polite, placing between her own face of abstract lines and the crude face of Little Flower, the insuperable distance of millennia" (*FT* 92).

Whereas people examine Little Flower's amazing smallness and supposed vulnerability with greedy interest, wanting to possess the miracle and even to use her as a servant or a pet, the small creature herself feels powerful and contented. Living constantly with the danger of being devoured by animals and members of other tribes, she experiences, as her epiphany, the triumph of having so far endured:

> She was laughing, warm, warm. . . . A laugh that the uncomfortable explorer did not succeed in classifying. And she went on enjoying her own gentle laugh, she who was not being devoured. Not to be devoured is the most perfect feeling. (*FT* 94)

Even her incipient motherhood will not lead her to confining bonds, for among the Likoualas a dubious practice prevails: "When a child is born, he is given his freedom almost at once" (*FT* 89). As her epiphany continues, Little Flower feels what "might be called love":

> She loved that sallow explorer. If she could have talked and told him that she loved him, he would have puffed up with vanity. A vanity that would have collapsed when she told him that she also loved the explorer's ring very much, and the explorer's boots. (*FT* 94)

Little Flower, unlike her urban counterparts, has no need to order and tame her chaotic desires; she merely enjoys them.

In answer to the explorer's question, Little Flower says it is "very nice to have a tree to live in that was hers, really hers. Because—and this she did not say but her eyes became so dark that they said it for her—because it is so nice to possess, so nice to possess" (*FT* 95). With the story of Little Flower, Lispector creates a comic parable of a native female power, sustained against all odds. The jungle inhabitant manages to retain the tranquil independence and unrepressed desires sought eagerly by city-bred women in their civilized world of enclosed spaces, prescribed behavior, and family ties. Lispector heaps on her protagonist multiple signs of powerlessness and oppression: membership in a black African tribe reminiscent of slavery and colonialism, the female sex, minute size, and the special dependence that pregnancy entails. She places her in opposition to a white male explorer (*explorador* in Portuguese means both "explorer" and "exploiter"). Yet the most vulnerable of women is not a victim. Unlike Laura, who cannot keep the roses, and unlike Lispector's other protagonists, who cannot hold on to and use their insights to change the forces that bind them, the smallest woman in the world, alone in her tree house, possesses herself—Lispector's wry symbol of an effective female power, though not of the means to attain it.

3
The Nurturing Text in Hélène Cixous and Clarice Lispector

> *She who looks with a look that recognizes, that studies, respects, doesn't take, doesn't claw, but attentively, with gentle relentlessness, contemplates and reads, caresses, bathes, makes the other gleam.*
>
> Hélène Cixous

I

"Who are you who are so strangely me?" Hélène Cixous asks, echoing an insistent inquiry she finds in Lispector's texts (Cixous 1991a, 169). This same question also animates Cixous's own fascinated scrutiny of Lispector. Her extensive readings include three books completely devoted to Lispector (*Vivre l'orange/To Live the Orange*, 1979b; *L'heure de Clarice Lispector* [1989, *The Hour of Clarice Lispector*]; and *Reading with Clarice Lispector*, 1990), as well as several articles and parts of books, forming a considerable body of writing that is remarkable on many counts.[1] Cixous's tender approach to the text of this woman, who is both other and not other with regard to herself, echoes Lispector's own preoccupation with the nuances of intersubjective relations, minutely analyzed by Cixous. Like Cixous, Lispector is a Jewish woman whose life was marked by immigration and the confluence of several languages. However, the kinship Cixous finds in Lispector goes far beyond these biographical circumstances. In Lispector's texts Cixous discerns consummate examples of *écriture féminine*, a kind of writing that Cixous defines as governed by a libidinal economy that favors spending, giving, and risk. As her label for it indicates, Cixous sees it as a feminine writing, although not as necessarily or exclusively authored by women. Cixous had been theorizing about *écriture féminine* for many years prior to her encounter with Lispector, without coming up with many examples of women writers who actually practiced it. If for Lispector's *oeuvre* Cixous's interest was most opportune, accelerating its translation into French and English and bringing it to wide international renown, for Cixous the discovery of Lispector was equally opportune, impelling her theorizing of *écriture féminine* and offering an example of a feminine libidinal economy authored by a woman.

Cixous's reception of Lispector inverts the usual colonial and postcolonial dynamic whereby Latin Americans translate and celebrate literatures from Europe and the United States. Even the wider circulation of Latin American texts in foreign literary markets since the 1960s has not changed radically this usually non-reciprocal dynamic. Inverting it, Cixous accords Lispector the highest praise, placing her repeatedly among the European writers that she particularly esteems, at times playing up her admiration with a teasing wit:

> If Kafka had been a woman. If Rilke had been a Jewish Brazilian born in the Ukraine. If Rimbaud had been a mother, if he had reached the age of fifty. If Heidegger had been able to stop being German, if he had written the Romance of the Earth. Why have I cited these names? To sketch out the general vicinity. Over there is where Clarice Lispector writes. There, where the most demanding works breathe, she makes her way. But then, at the point where the philosopher gets winded, she goes on, further still than all knowledge. (Cixous 1991a, 132)

Cixous not only celebrates Lispector, but also claims that the Brazilian had a decisive impact in the development of her own work. Thus, Lispector is perhaps the only Latin American writer other than Borges to have been singled out by a European writer as a significant model or inspiration. Of course, the collapsing of hierarchical oppositions (feminine/masculine, Latin American/ European, Portuguese language/French) is part of the point of this celebration, making Lispector ideologically most appropriate for Cixous's attentions. What better way to dramatize Cixous's own openness to the other, to the other woman, than to divulge the text, written by a little-known foreign woman, a text that not only offers an example of a female-authored feminine libidinal economy, but also provides the opportunity for a feminine reception by Cixous herself? What better evidence for the existence of a transculturally feminine libidinal economy than to find it, plain and clear, in a woman's words in an exotic language? This fortuitous appropriateness, and the admiration and perceived kinship that attract any writer to another, have combined to form an extraordinarily persistent fascination, for

Cixous has taught and written about Lispector steadily since she first came to know of the Brazilian writer in the late 1970s.

Several critics—Carol Ambruster, Verena Conley, Anne Rosalind Jones, Toril Moi, Susan Rubin Suleiman, and Morag Shiach, among others—have discussed Cixous's writing about Lispector in an attempt to understand what the Brazilian novelist has meant for Cixous. I would like to pursue instead the reciprocal perspective, and ask about the pertinence of Cixous's reading to an understanding of Lispector. Practicing a form of commentary that is far from traditional or academic literary criticism, in her readings of Lispector and of other writers—Kleist, Rilke, Joyce, Kafka, Genet, as well as Lacan and Derrida, who often served as her points of departure—Cixous works out her own theoretical and ethical concerns. Her writings nevertheless paint a portrait—many portraits—of Lispector. "For more than ten years now, H.C. has been teaching and writing about Clarice, painting the same head over and over—nor is she finished yet," Susan Suleiman writes (Suleiman 1991, xiv). What, we may ask, are the contours of this likeness? How do the attention, respect, and gentle stubbornness of Cixous's gaze frame the Brazilian author, and what are the implications of this gaze?

The critics who have discussed Cixous's readings of Lispector have avoided a probing critique, and it is indeed difficult to do otherwise. Cixous's passionate reading, shading into the homoerotic, and its celebration of a woman and of the feminine, will be at least partly attractive to any feminist, and admirers of Lispector will appreciate Cixous's sustained effort to claim for the Brazilian writer the audience she deserves. Moreover, Cixous's defense of intuition as the route to a superior knowledge—a preference she shares with Lispector—challenges a critic's attempt to understand the logic and implications of her mode of reading. In her essay "The Author in Truth" (discussed below), Cixous denounces "the trap of critical interpellation," that inner and outer demand for proofs, for explanation. "Explain the inexplicable," she counters:

> Either you know without knowing, and this unknowing knowledge is a flash of joy the other shares with you, or else there is nothing. You'll never convert someone who is not already converted. You'll never touch a heart planted on another planet. (Cixous 1991a, 158)

Many of Cixous's critics have effectively illuminated aspects of her writing by staying within the sphere of sympathy and intersubjective attunement. Susan R. Suleiman, for instance, at the end of her introduction to a collection of Cixous's essays recently published in English, is drawn into the mirroring economy of some of Cixous's texts: "Who has spoken here? A 'Jewoman' living and writing in a language that is not her mother tongue, in a country that is not the country of her birth: S.R.S." (Suleiman 1991, xxii). Yet the risk of seeming to be "a heart planted on another planet" is, I think, worth taking. The difficulty of assuming a critical position indeed points to a disturbing aspect in Cixous's readings of Lispector: their self-positioning as a closed, intuitive dialogue between kindred souls engaged in a mutual exchange, emphasized by Cixous's titles and subtitles: *Reading with Clarice Lispector*; "Letting Oneself (be) Read (by) Clarice Lispector" (1991b). One need not take this mutuality literally to see that it in fact represses the appropriative nature of the critical act, performed by necessity on an unconsenting patient, the writer's text. Cixous's attempt to counter that appropriation by imagining in its place a "dialogue" with the (dead) author only increases it, I think, by implying a privileged position for her own critical discourse: Lispector accompanies and authorizes my readings, she reads me as much as I read her. This fervent "dialogue," which allows no outside voices—it is telling that Cixous never mentions what any third party has said about Lispector—ultimately gives the false impression that Lispector is a sort of Cixousian twin: to quote Susan Suleiman again, "two authors who are not one, but who are very, very close" (1991, xv). Without claiming an impossible impartiality, and without denying the marked Cixous-Lispector kinship, I would argue that it is worth suspending sympathy in order to question (from another planet) some of Cixous's moves in presenting Lispector.

II

My commentary—necessarily selective, as Cixous's readings of Lispector are by now extensive—focuses on representative texts, following the development of the paradoxical basis that sustains them: the apparent openness to the alterity of the other and of the text that at the same time implies a mirroring of Cixous and of *écriture féminine* in Lispector. Cixous's two initial texts, *Vivre l'orange / To live the Orange* and "Clarice Lispector: The Approach," both first published in 1979, are of special interest because they narrate, one as fiction/autobiography and the other as critical essay, Cixous's discovery of this *oeuvre* that would attract her so profoundly. Although in a footnote to the article Cixous states that it is "a moment taken" from the book (Cixous 1979a, 409), the two differ in interesting ways.

In *To live the Orange*, a lyrical narrative in which fiction and autobiography intertwine, a first-person narrator tells about the epiphanic revelations produced by her initial reading of Lispector. The plot recurrently revisits that magical originary scene, told with shifting mythic subtexts and metaphors. "A woman's voice came to me from far away," Cixous writes:

> Like a voice from a birth town, it brought me insights I once had, intimate insights, naive and knowing, ancient and fresh like the yellow and violet color of freshias rediscovered, this voice was unknown to me, it reached me on the twelfth of October 1978, this voice was not searching for me, it

was writing to no one, to all women, to writing, in a foreign tongue, I do
not speak it, but my heart understands it, and its silent words in all the
veins of my life have translated themselves into mad blood, into joy-
blood.[2]

"Discovered" on the same day, October 12, that Columbus discovered America, Lispector opens up a New World, bringing a renewal of energy and innocence to Cixous, whose disillusionment and depleted writing are later likened to a Europe ravaged by wars and History. This discovery is also, however, a rediscovery and Lispector's newness is also ancient. Another layer of mythic subtexts likens Lispector's writing to a nurturing Mother Earth, or a pre-Oedipal mother, who brings back a lost harmony:

A writing found me when I was unfindable to myself. More than a writing,
the great writing, the writing of other days, the terrestrial, vegetal writing,
of the time when the earth was the sovereign mother, the good mistress,
and we went to the school of growth in her countries. (*TLO* 12)

The paradise lost that Lispector represents is a garden of the word, of innocent naming that reveals the true essence of things:

How to call forth claricely: it's a long and passionate work for all the
senses. Going, approaching, grazing, abiding, touching, calling-in,
presenting, — giving, — taking. Calling things forth, this is her work, giving
things back to things, giving us each thing for the first time, giving us
back each time the first time of things. (*TLO* 104)

In whatever guise Lispector appears—and she is angel, nymph, nature, mother, as well as *amie*, a participant in an exchange of erotic woman-to-woman love—she is always all giving. While revealing and giving the orange, the apple, the leaf, the rose, Lispector becomes each of these in turn, in metaphors that slip and shift. Although this brief account does not exhaust Cixous's rich and varied strategies of rhetorical figuration, it is enough to point up the paradoxical nature of her presentation of Lispector. Whereas on the surface Cixous offers Lispector praise, warmth, and a generous receptivity—a nurturing text modeled after the very pattern she ascribes to Lispector—she also silences Lispector by muting and replacing her words.

It is perhaps the point of Cixous's fictional presentation of Lispector to make her into a presence that fits exactly the measure of Cixous's need: she appears only as filtered through the subjectivity of an autobiographical narrator. Although the remarkable inflections of Lispector's voice are what attract Cixous, her voice is absorbed into Cixous's text: quotations are almost entirely omitted, buried, or transformed. In *To live the Orange*, which focuses relentlessly on Lispector's impact on Cixous, there is only one brief acknowledged quotation, vaguely introduced by the words: "The original sentence said, it seems to me . . . " (*TLO* 38). The text, however, does include a number of blurred quotations, in which Cixous paraphrases recognizable passages from Lispector without acknowledging her move, and what might be called simulated quotations, in which the words set off in italics might seem to be Lispector's, but are Cixous's own paraphrases and conflations of several Lispector texts. In one instance, Cixous combines the apple, a symbolic object in Lispector's longest novel, *The Apple in the Dark* (1967), with the inquisitive mode, the insistence upon fresh perception of ordinary objects, and the birdlike, flying, and alighting egg from the short story "The Egg and the Chicken." The resulting amalgam is set off as if it were a quotation:

> Clarice gives on to an apple. The apple grows bigger, and falls before us with the supple strength of a bird, and while with a calm movement it comes to alight upon the window-sill, its flight makes us think around it with wonder: "Is it possible that I have thought no more of an apple since the beginning of the century? And that I have not seen an apple, not discovered, not observed an apple when scarcely emerged from its element, still stirred, aerial, it changes its nature in alightening on the table? And becomes stone, or becomes egg?" (*TLO* 80)

The passage Cixous puts in quotation marks contains a tone and topics taken from Lispector, but it is ascribed to plural witnesses, the readers of Lispector, thereby blurring the demarcations between Cixous and Lispector, reader and writer. The "I" is Lispector, but also Cixous and the readers of Lispector and Cixous. Elsewhere in the text, Cixous indirectly ascribes her own words to Lispector by writing them in Portuguese; when she also writes in Italian and Spanish, she lends the words a polylingual resonance rarely seen in Lispector.

It is worth remarking that the orange, Cixous's central symbolic object, representative of herself, of Lispector, of all women, is mentioned casually once or twice but is never made much of in any of Lispector's texts. It had, however, appeared in an earlier novel by Cixous, *Portrait du soleil* (1973), as Morag Shiach observes, where it is written " 'oranje,' a combination of Cixous's place of birth Oran, and the first person pronoun 'je' " (Shiach 1991, 79). In *To live the Orange*, Cixous refers to what she calls "voluntary translation" as a partly guilt-ridden and appropriative, partly joyful, act, assertive both of a challenge to herself and of a collaborative enterprise among women: "In the translation of the apple (into orange) I try to denounce myself. A way of owning. My part. Of the fruit. Of the enjoyment. Of venturing to say that which I am not yet in a position to ensure by my own care" (*TLO* 40). Because part of the resonance of the orange for Cixous is that the word contains the name of her own city of birth, Oran (in Algeria), Lispector, by giving Cixous the orange, figuratively reconnects her to her origins. Cixous also insists on Lispector's Jewishness, a mirror of her own heritage, embodied in the (reinvented) material signs of the fruit: "oranjuive," "oranjew." What Cixous receives from Lispector, then, as symbolized in the orange, is not a reaching out toward alterity, but rather a mirroring of self and sameness.

Cixous's assimilation of Lispector is neatly paralleled by what Cixous reads as Lispector's movement toward selflessness, toward shedding "the membrane of self" (*TLO* 36). In a passage reminiscent of an eerie dream scene in Ingmar Bergman's *The Hour of the Wolf*, Cixous imagines Lispector peeling off layers of her face like so many masks:

> I saw her take off this face, a cry rose in my throat, she did it so quickly, I saw the second face, it was a non-face, without an eyebrow, without an eye, I didn't have time to be struck, to cry out, for the process went on, excessively fast, she defaced the non-face, the third was pale but matt, the eyebrow thinner, sharper, the eyes absorbed in observing the object, that was done swiftly, the gestures too rapid for me to be able to see them happen, I saw the Face de-face itself. (*TLO* 50)

Faceless, possessed of "torrential alterability" (*TLO* 51), Lispector's text blends with Cixous's own writing to form a chorus with the writing of all women, revealing Cixous to herself and sustaining her capacity to write. A similar diminishing of the self, the better to nurture and fuel other selves, occurs in a strange passage where Cixous seems to absolve Lispector of having teeth, that is, of any violence or aggression: "A being at whom Clarice had been smiling for fifteen years, for whom she was but a smile, had never seen her teeth" (*TLO* 106). In order to ensure that Lispector be all gentleness, all giving, Cixous makes Lispector the object of self-disfiguring, self-effacing gestures.

The issue of appropriation points to the central paradox in Cixous's use of Lispector. Ann Jones has observed that in *To live the Orange*, Cixous celebrates "women's pre-conceptual, non-appropriative openness to people and to objects, to the other within and outside them" (Jones 1985, 89). The mode of this celebration, however, rests on a disquieting erasure and appropriation of another woman's words. That woman's otherness is entirely disallowed and effaced to the extent that it does not coincide with the feminine libidinal economy that Cixous charges her with representing. Cixous's openness is open only to elements of sameness, not alterity. To seek in a foreign woman extensions of one's own self, as well as the dismembered and repressed "foreign parts of the self" (*TLO* 28), serves as a puzzling instance of a respectful and nonappropriative literary reception.

Borrowing terms from Gayatri Spivak's critique of Julia Kristeva's *About Chinese Women*, one might object to Cixous's use of Lispector's texts merely to ask and answer questions about her own identity, avoiding "the necessary other focus: not merely who am I? but who is the other woman? How am I naming her?

How does she name me?" (Spivak 1981, 179). Although the textual procedures that Cixous underlines under the rubric of *écriture féminine* can indeed be found in Lispector—hence the strength of her interpretation—Lispector's writing is not limited to them. In *To live the Orange*, the surface plot, which shows Cixous joyfully receiving and imitating Lispector, disguises the erasure and replacement of Lispector's more ample, heterogeneous, and contradictory text with what seems like a mirror image of Cixous's own writing.

Cixous's article "Clarice Lispector: The Approach" repeats the motifs of approach and mutual interpenetration, as the title and two subtitles suggest: "Letting Oneself (be) Read (by) Clarice Lispector, The Passion according to C.L." Although it maintains a lyrical undertow, this essay moves closer to the conventions of literary criticism by making explicit Cixous's theoretical lineage. Erudite references, quotations, and even sly parodies of philosophers and poets, mainly Heidegger, Derrida, and Rilke, are incorporated into the flow of Cixous's lyrical celebration. Yet the text remains almost fictional. Characters engage in a mutually enriching interchange: Cixous, representing every woman—a "we" that is occasionally reduced to an "I"—reads "writing-a-woman," the womanly writing of Lispector.[3]

In "Clarice Lispector's Approach," reading and writing are accomplished under the sign of an exuberant femininity. As Ann Jones points out, Cixous rejects Freudian and Lacanian theories of woman as lack: "[Cixous] calls for an assertion of the female body as plenitude, as a positive force, the source simultaneously of multiple physical capacities (gestation, birth, lactation) and of liberating texts" (Jones 1985, 8). In the wake of charges of essentialism, the terms "masculine" and "feminine" have become vexed ones for Cixous, used in quotation marks and accompanied by many caveats. In a 1982 interview, and elsewhere, she insists on the cultural construction of femininity, claiming that libidinal femininity is not present necessarily or exclusively in texts written by women and that, similarly, a libidinal masculinity does not depend on the biological sex of the writer. She goes on to say that "in spite of everything and for historical reasons, the economy said to be feminine . . . characterized by features, by traits, which are more adventurous, more on the side of spending, riskier, on the side of the body, is more livable in women than in men" (Conley 1984, 133). For Cixous, Lispector "is a woman who says things as closely as possible to a feminine economy, that is to say, one of the greatest generosity possible, of the greatest virtue, of the greatest spending" (Conley 1984, 155). Cixous pits Lispector's feminine economy against economies present in writers such as Rilke, Kafka, and Joyce, who, as Cixous would say, happen to be male. Lispector functions, for Cixous, as a prime example of a libidinal femininity written by a woman.

In Cixous's dense and shifting metaphorical web that characterizes Lispector, metaphors that present her as mediator predominate and repeat the theme of access to the other: the Clarice-school, the Clarice-voice, the Clarice-window. Clarice not only approaches the other, but also teaches us the right approach. The effects of Clarice's text are likened to procreation and organic growth, and she becomes fruit and flower, offering herself to another's sensual enjoyment. Reading-writing in this essay is synonymous with giving-receiving, terms that are also reversible and entirely implicated one in the other.

If Lispector gives and receives object lessons, Cixous, in analogous fashion, gives and receives Lispector lessons. The benevolent exchange that Cixous observes between Lispector and objects repeats itself in the exchange between Cixous and Lispector. Here both Lispector and Cixous enact the role of Melanie Klein's Good Mother that Toril Moi also finds privileged elsewhere in Cixous: "the omnipotent and generous giver of love, nourishment and plenitude" (Moi 1985, 115).

Cixous's presentation of Lispector rests, then, on a deep, though questionable, sympathy. Using the words of another woman from a foreign place, Cixous establishes a tender dialogue, and discerns in them multiple mirrorings of the dynamics of her own texts and a representative of a feminine libidinal economy. As a superlative reader of the nuances of gentleness in Lispector, Cixous both describes and enacts the generative receptivity toward objects and beings she finds in Lispector. The following passage, which again glosses Lispector's short story "The Egg and the Chicken," can serve as example of this complex mixture of assimilation, imitation, and praise, so frequent in this essay:

> A patience pays attention. An attention that is terse, active, discreet, warm, almost imperceptible, imponderable like a light rekindling of looks,
> regular, twenty-one days and twenty-one nights, at the kitchen window, and at last an egg is. They pay attention: doing nothing, not upsetting, filling, replacing, taking up the space. Leaving the space alone. Thinking
> delicately of. Directing the mixture of knowing looks and loving light towards. A face. Surrounding it with a discreet, confident, attentive questioning, attuning to, watching over it, for a long time, until penetrating into the essence. (CLA 66)

Enticing as the flow of Cixous's lyrical gentleness may be, I find some of its implications disturbing with regard to Cixous's own critical strategy. Although celebrating in Lispector a nonappropriative gaze that casts light, warms, reveals but does not upset, Cixous ignores the appropriative implications of "penetrating into the essence" when this is done, as she seems to be doing here, as a method of textual criticism: it arrests the play of meanings, of interpretations and reinterpretations, with the fixity of a purported "truth." The "truth" she finds in Lispector is compromised and limited by Cixous's own need for her to typify a feminine libidinal economy manifested in traditional feminine stereotypes of the Nurturing Woman: woman as mediator, as benevolent nature, as Good Mother. Although this is not a misreading—certain elements in Lispector's texts may be profitably read in this way—such an interpretation diminishes and restricts the more ample dynamics of a text that can observe just as intensely harsh interactions and can itself be unsparing and aggressive toward the reader.

Cixous, along with Irigaray and Kristeva, has often engaged in revalorizing the traditionally feminine, yet that revalorization remains problematic. Domna Stanton questions what she calls the maternal metaphor in Cixous, Irigaray, and Kristeva: "woman as/is mother" (Stanton 1986, 159). In their "maternal metaphorizations," when these three writers "countervalorize the traditional antithesis that identifies man with culture and confines woman to instinctual nature," they "reproduce the dichotomy between male rationality and female materiality, corporeality and sexuality, which Irigaray has traced to Plato and Plotinus" (Stanton 1986, 170). "[T]he devalued term in phallologic becomes the superior value but the system of binary oppositions remains the same" (Stanton 1986, 170). Cixous's writing about Lispector maintains those old dichotomies and limits the Brazilian writer to the set of traits on the feminine side, countervalued though they may be. This agenda, I would claim, is Cixous's rather than Lispector's. It is not surprising that Cixous's reading is biased and reductive because all readings to some extent must be. One can, nevertheless, object to its elaborate, although implicit, claim to escape bias and reductiveness through the agency of a nonobtrusive, nondominating gaze. The nurturing gentleness Cixous finds so repeatedly and exclusively in Lispector's texts and uses as her own method of reading, like a disguised straitjacket, ties Lispector to a limited interpretation. Moreover, the superior authorization that Cixous, in her readings, seems to claim, derives from the Cixous–Lispector mirroring that her mode of reading itself produces.

Cixous's main concern in "Clarice Lispector: The Approach" goes beyond an interpretation of Lispector and beyond the autobiographical/fictional account of one reader's encounter with a transforming text that she offers in *To live the Orange*. The article defends and exemplifies more sharply the possibilities of a wider cultural transformation wrought by *écriture féminine*. Lispector's patient and womanly "science of the other," "an art in itself," demonstrates "all the ways of letting all the beings with their different strangenesses enter our proximity" (CLA 66) and heralds a mode of writing/reading that will allow women to come into writing, into greater cultural visibility. "There must be a wait so powerfully thoughtful, open, toward beings so close, so womanly-familiar that they are forgotten for it, so that the day will come in which women who have always been-there, will at last appear" (CLA 77). Those of us interested in Cixous's account of Lispector would do well to note its blind spots as well as the aspects of Lispector's texts—familiar, forgotten, invisible—that Cixous foregrounds and articulates, illuminating by her powerful *parti pris*.

I will now turn to two essays published much later, in 1987 and 1989. Although the Cixous–Lispector mirroring continues in these texts, as does the modeling of Cixous's critical text on certain aspects of Lispector's fictional text, Cixous modifies her earlier approach significantly, both in the expansion of the corpus of Lispector's writing to which she refers and in the increasingly liberal use of quotations, including some in the Portuguese.

I might mention here that Cixous's apparent command of Portuguese is not entirely adequate to the task of interpreting the nuances of Lispector's texts. A curious sort of stylistic commentary crops up, especially in her seminars of the early 1980s transcribed in *Reading with Clarice Lispector*, where Cixous makes a point of mentioning Portuguese words or grammatical constructions, but then interprets them in their deviations or implications for the French ear. "In Portuguese, 'understand' is 'hear' " (Cixous 1991b, 56). It is not the Portuguese *entender*, however, but the French *entendre* that has the double meaning of perception through both the intelligence and the sense of hearing. This is not an isolated slip, but an instance of a rather cavalier and Francocentric attitude toward the letter of Lispector's text, even as she examines it in detail. She often makes much of Lispector's omission of the first-person subject pronoun, the norm in Portuguese (unless one wants to give special emphasis to the performer of the action), and reads it as the significant deviation it would be if it occurred in French (or English). "Clarice writes in order to dissolve through a certain chemistry, through a certain magic and love, that which would be retention, weight, solidification, an arrest of the act of writing. That is why she ends by dropping the subject pronoun and saying: What am I saying? Am saying love" (Cixous 1991b, 69). In Portuguese, Lispector could hardly do otherwise. Cixous, even in her attention to Lispector's words, is in many instances unable (or unwilling) to tune in to the real otherness of the language, an attitude she repeats in her disregard for textual structures of greater interpretive moment.

Cixous's essay "Reaching the Point of Wheat, or A Portrait of the Artist as a Maturing Woman," uses the concepts of feminine and masculine libidinal economies to examine fictional accounts of the formation of the artist. The article pursues "a kind of meditation on creation and perhaps also on the different attitudes that men and women show with regard to becoming an artist" (Cixous 1987b, 1).[4] Although Cixous warns the reader against taking the terms "man" and "woman" too literally and insists on the cultural construction of gender, here male writers exemplify the masculine and female writers the feminine libidinal economies: "Joyce, in order to illustrate what I feel about the artist as a young man, and Clarice Lispector, because of what she has to say about women. And it happens that he is a man and she is a woman. . . . What I am interested in is the libidinal education of the artist, that is, what in his/her libidinal structure, in his/her affective, in his/her psychic structure is going to be determined particularly by sexual difference" (RPW 1-2).

Cixous's argument pits the feminine transgression of the Law, "the non-fear of knowing what is inside" and "knowing through pleasure" (RPW, 2-3), against a masculine timidity and a respect for the Law, which harks back to the fear of castration. She weaves in commentaries on the story of Eve, on a medieval quest story, on Joyce's *Portrait of the Artist as a Young Man*, on Kafka's parable "Before the Law," and on Lispector's first novel, *Near to the Wild Heart*. She reserves the most detailed commentary for Lispector. Even with ample use of quotations from an expanded number of Lispector's stories and novels, and a more nuanced, varied, and inclusive view of Lispector's many textures, Cixous nevertheless still holds her to a stable position as a "model of 'feminine' writings" (RPW 9). Furthermore, she insists on the maternal relation of the female author to the reader:

> Clarice is going to lead us on a quest for the truth of existence—the truth of life, which is something very difficult. In a way she will become a kind of mother. Of course this is idealistic, since not all mothers are good. But what she becomes is a kind of mother of creation, a kind of mother of life, and this will consist of what she calls *taking care of things* very carefully. She will finally elaborate a kind of philosophy, or even a kind of set of morals. (RPW 14)

In the last seven pages of the article, Cixous unfolds a subtle reading of four short texts by Lispector ("Clandestine Felicity," "The Foreign Legion," "The Partaking of the Bread," and "So Much Mansuetude"). In them, Cixous finds instances of Lispector's exemplary approaches to the object of desire: "the art of having what we have," "the art of keeping alive," "the art of blessing," and, finally, "the art of receiving: the point of wheat." Again, what counts for Cixous in Lispector are the moments "when one is courageous enough to drop the heavy self and open to the other" (RPW 18) and a libidinal economy that gives without asking for anything in return. In a final paragraph that blends Lispector's words with her own, the "I" of the critic underwrites, merges with, and expands on the novelist's words:

> No paying except attention. Being alive without asking for thanks, just looking with beneficent eyes. One really has to make a big effort, and particularly one has to overrule the ego and the pretense of mastering things and knowing things. Then we reach the point when we can say as she says: it is only because I don't know anything in an appropriating way, "because I don't know anything and because I remember nothing," because I am not a prisoner of the past and I am not a captive of the future, "and because it is night, then I stretch out my hand and I save the child." The serene and joyful hand of the artist saves the child, any child, and signs: Am Alive. (RPW 20)

Cixous's dichotomy between the positive feminine libidinal economy and the negative masculine one has consequences, I believe, for what she sees and what she ignores in Lispector's narratives. In her commentary, she mostly elides plot, focusing instead on moments of lyrical perception, and assimilates most characters, especially those who speak in the first person, to versions of Lispector. She makes Lispector's protagonists, and Lispector herself, into epitomes of wisdom, placing them in a "serene and joyful" utopian realm. When narrative involves the creation of characters and plots by an "author" who manipulates them in order to tell a "truth," it necessarily entails "the pretense of mastering things and knowing things," even knowing in an appropriative way. In Lispector's tension-ridden, conflictive texts, the narrative enacts struggles between characters; between authorial surrogates, narrators, and their creatures; between the writer as "seer" into the heart of things and the writer as victim of compelling unconscious forces. The result is a fictional imagination that is not as sweet and nurturing as Cixous implies. We see Cixous, then, freezing and magnifying moments of Lispector's texts, and taking these parts for the whole. She frames Lispector by means of two complementary critical moves: the metaphorical move of equating all of Lispector's writing to maternal nurturance, and the metonymic move of isolating lyrical moments, stripping them of their conflictive contexts. Although these are commonplace moves in textual criticism, and Cixous is an excellent reader of her chosen moments of Lispector, her interpretation is misleadingly narrow.

The last essay I will discuss, "The Author in Truth" (entitled "Extrême fidélité" in a previous version), a long and complex piece, repeats and revises certain passages from "Reaching the Point of Wheat," and also places them in a context that encompasses still more of Lispector's texts.[5] Cixous cites textual instances that challenge, even threaten and thereby expand, her previous reading — for example, Lispector's use of a masculine narrator in *The Hour of the Star* — and quotes more amply, including a long quotation in the original Portuguese. The essay discusses relations between author, narrator, and character in *The Hour of the Star*, with detours into other texts ("Clandestine Felicity," "The Foreign Legion," *The Passion according to G.H.*, and "Such Gentleness") that highlight Lispector's feminine relations to the other and to desire. Metaphors for her own reading of Lispector again evoke nurturance and imitate Lispector's openness to the other: "What follows is a modest meditation on this book [*The Hour of the Star*] which is born of books so that it can totter into our hearts like a child" (AT 140). In the initial version, the "extreme faithfulness" of the title refers to Clarice's respect for the otherness of the other, a respect that Cixous herself purports to echo in her reception of Clarice. I quote the first sentence (in brackets), which is omitted in the revised version, because it makes explicit the parallel between Cixous and Lispector:

> [The greatest respect that I have for any *oeuvre* in the world, that's the respect I have for the *oeuvre* of Clarice Lispector.] The work of Clarice

Lispector stages all the possible positions of the pleasuring subject in his or her relation to acts of appropriation. Scenes of use and abuse of ownership. And she has done this through the most subtle and delicate details. The text struggles endlessly against the movement of appropriation, which, even in its most innocent guises, is fatally destructive. Isn't pity destructive? Badly thought out love is destructive; ill-measured understanding is annihilating. We think we are holding out a hand? We hit. The work of Clarice Lispector is an immense book of respect. Book of the right distance. (Cixous 1987a, 24; AT 155-56)

We see, then, that Cixous discusses issues that are vital to literary criticism — appropriation, respect, understanding, distance — as they refer to the movements of Lispector's text, while silently passing over their pertinence to her own critical text. Cixous points out that "the most difficult thing to do is to arrive at the most extreme proximity while guarding against the trap of projection, of identification. The other must remain absolutely strange within the greatest possible proximity" (AT 170-71). Cixous claims that Lispector achieves this delicate balance. I would argue that Cixous does not avoid the trap of identification, since an instance of it is the mirroring effect so prevalent in her readings.

A predictable outcome of Cixous's refusal to recognize the inevitable appropriations of the critical act is her need to save Lispector from other critics, whose readings do not corroborate Cixous's "truths." This would be an instance of the trap of projection, in the Freudian sense of "the attribution to another . . . of qualities, feelings or wishes that the subject repudiates or refuses to recognize in himself" (Laplanche and Pontalis 1973, 352). Cixous's own appropriation of Lispector entails an odd sort of self-effacement and a projection of the appropriative act onto others, as we can see in a passage from "Extrême Fidélité," which was cut from the later version:

> I would never have another seminar if I knew that enough people read Clarice Lispector. A few years ago when they began to divulge her, I said to myself: I will no longer have a seminar, you only need to read her, everything is said, it's perfect. But everything became repressed as usual, and they have even transformed her in an extraordinary way, embalmed her, stuffed her with straw in the guise of a Brazilian bourgeoise with polished fingernails. So I continue to accompany her with a reading that watches over her. (Cixous 1987a, 26)

Cixous forestalls false transformations by overseeing the true one, which will fix Lispector as a writer of the French *féminine* and save Lispector even from herself, from her historical context and her class. For she was, of course, a Brazilian bourgeoise among other things; she even looked like one. Her conspicuously painted lips, large pieces of jewelry, and made-up eyes confront us from many of her photographs. There is, then, a disguised authoritarianism in Cixous's treatment of Lispector. One could say of Cixous what a beleaguered son says of his controlling mother in Lispector's short story "Happy Birthday": "A mother's love [is] difficult to bear" (Lispector 1972, 85).

Because Cixous offers powerful readings of Lispector, bringing into sharp relief important configurations in her text while also performing the enormous service of calling international attention to the Brazilian writer's work, it is important, I think, to see as well the confining implications of Cixous's interpretation. Her reading, which "watches over" Lispector, should not be allowed to protect her from other imaginative assaults, other appropriations, for, as Cixous well knows, but seems to forget, no one critic holds any one key to an author's writing (even if she is a Brazilian writing in Portuguese).

III

In order to question Cixous's exclusive focus in her readings of Lispector on textual interactions that privilege the link between writing and nurturing, I will turn to a short story, "The Egg and the Chicken," from the collection *The Foreign Legion* (Lispector 1964, trans. 1986),[6] a fascinating if enigmatic parable about the relation between creators and their *oeuvres*. Here we find a link between nurturing and writing that is fraught with irony, conflict, and contradictory investments, revealing a Lispector who differs significantly from Cixous's wise and gentle mother.

Cixous's discussion of this story in "The Egg and the Chicken: Love Is Not Having" (Cixous 1990) focuses on a different portion of the artistic transaction, the relation between the text and the reader. She develops homologies between seeing the egg, loving a person, and reading a text, and extracts Lispector's teachings in these areas: "It is a lesson of the egg as well as of the look. It is a lesson of love and reading" (Cixous 1990, 102). Like all of Cixous's published seminars, this is not as tightly organized as her essays written for publication. Verena Conley suggests helpfully that "the seminars can be read as laboratory for Cixous's fictional and critical practices" (Conley 1991, ix). However, the winding paths of this seminar's progression can be seen to have a critical purpose, if we apply to Cixous's rambling method what she says of Lispector's discontinous attention to the egg: "Occupied to [*sic*] awake over the egg and at the same time distracted, the value of which is important in Clarice: when one is not distracted, one starts appropriating and it's all over. One has to be attentively superficial and distracted" (Cixous 1990, 121). It is at least debatable whether a critic's distraction can actually protect the text she reads from appropriation. (It could be argued that a wandering attention could instead allow us to replace the supposed object of our scrutiny with our own habitual fantasies and concerns.) Whether tersely, as in her essays, or more diffusely, as in this seminar, Cixous returns to the questions that always haunt her in Lispector, including the superior wisdom of an exemplary relation to the other, a lesson that her own critical text seeks to absorb and duplicate. Her statement about Lispector's approach to the egg can also be applied to her approach to Lispector's text: "One never seizes the egg. One never arrives at it. The egg remains unseizable. Then you have it and then you don't" (Cixous 1990, 105).

If not seizing, for Cixous, is a crucial requisite for understanding, not giving and not having are equally requisites for loving. "I accompany the egg to another text, 'Felicidade Clandestina' (Secret Happiness), which I did not want to introduce right away. If I do not give it right away, it is out of love. Not to give something right away is perhaps one of the definitions of love" (Cixous 1990, 116). The loving care for her reader, and the loving reading of Lispector, are, for Cixous, lessons learned from Lispector's parable: "In my opinion, all stories about eggs are stories of love" (Cixous 1990, 103).

Whereas Cixous draws lessons on how to read from Lispector's approach to the egg ("Any subtle text is some kind of egg, an object that can be placed only with absolute caution" [Cixous 1990, 104]), I would like to turn to the text's meditation not on the relation between readers and texts but on the relation between artistic producers and what they produce. If the chicken is an emblem of single-minded maternal concern, the egg can be a prototype of what needs to be nurtured. As Cixous observes, "It is a form that presents itself as having to be nonviolated" (Cixous 1990, 103). In this story, the intersection of nurturing, female gender, and writing foregrounds the identification of writing with motherly nurture, but also questions it. A female first-person narrator, mother and writer, takes up two simultaneous activities. First, she performs a free-ranging, verbally exuberant meditation on the egg, the chicken, and their relation. These signifiers accrue meanings that at first seem to shift with dizzying abandon, but soon cohere into recurring topics. Second, in a fragmented sequence that slowly unfolds throughout the story, the narrator breaks eggs into a frying pan and supervises her children's breakfast.

This story engages the contradictions and continuities inherent in the simultaneous occupation of the positions of the provider of nourishment and purveyor of texts. The "oneiric verbal fantasy," as one critic terms it (Nunes 1973, 88), that begins the story takes off from a commonplace domestic sight: "In the morning, I see the egg on the kitchen table" (*FL* 47). Definitions of the egg, divergent in tone and context, follow fast upon one another, at a clipped, breathless pace. The verbal play turns on aphoristic formulations ("Upon seeing an egg it is already too late: an egg seen is an egg lost" [*FL* 47]), parodies of philosophical discourse ("Do I know the egg? It is almost certain that I do. Like this: I exist, therefore I know" [*FL* 49]), paradoxes ("To see the egg is impossible: the egg is supervisible, just as there are supersonic sounds" [*FL* 47]), and fanciful absurdities ("The moon is inhabited by eggs" [*FL* 48]). A more solemn mythic language introduces two strange identifications: of the narrator with the chicken, and of the egg with a work of art (or *l'oeuf d'art*, as Cixous puts it, [Cixous 1979a, 413]):

> When I was ancient, I was the depositary of an egg and I walked softly to avoid disturbing the egg's silence. When I died, they carefully removed the egg from inside me. It was still alive. (*FL* 47)

Meditation on the egg gives way to a consideration of the chicken's generative and protective role. The egg—fragile, fleeting, and elusive in nature—is a mysterious, weightless presence, taking on the attributes of a bird or even of the Holy Spirit in its birdlike guise. Whereas the egg displays its perfect form, the chicken is clumsy in design: "As for the chicken's body, the chicken's body is the clearest proof that the egg does not exist. It is enough to look at the chicken to see that the egg cannot possibly exist" (*FL* 49). An ironic parable of artistic creation weaves in and out of this text: a Kafkian parable, opaque, at times self-contradictory, without transparent correspondences or predictable development. It stresses the disparate, incommensurate natures of creators and their artifacts, which they shape but do not control: "The egg is the soul of the chicken. The awkward chicken. The impeccable egg. The terrified chicken. The impeccable egg. Like a stationary missile" (*FL* 48). For Lispector, the egg with its superior power comes first, visiting upon the chicken its uninvited and demanding presence: "As for what came first, it was the egg that discovered the chicken. The chicken was not even summoned. The chicken is chosen spontaneously" (*FL* 50).

The narrator and the chicken coincide not only in their maternal position, but also in their lack of understanding of the egg. The chicken's dim wit shades into the narrator's privileged suspension of the rational faculty, which allows other forms of knowledge to emerge:

> When the chicken sees the egg, she thinks that she is dealing with something impossible. And with her heart beating, with her heart beating furiously, she fails to recognize the egg. Suddenly, I look at the egg in the kitchen and all I see there is something to eat. I fail to recognize it and my heart is beating. (*FL* 51)

Although she is a female creature and one whose traits include a caricature of submissive and self-sacrificing maternity and domesticity, the chicken gains here the status of a generically inclusive figure for any artist, male or female. Lispector's chicken creates the egg, offering it an instinctive, although noncomprehending protection, and only occasionally balks at her self-effacing role. However, in the last two pages of the story, the chicken disappears. The narrator takes over the chicken's function in caring for the egg and admits to her membership in a secret society:

I belong to the freemasonry of those who have seen the egg once and then deny it as a means of ensuring its protection. We are those who refrain from destroying and in this consume our lives. Agents in disguise, . . . occasionally we recognize each other. (*FL* 52)

The agents (masculine in Portuguese, *os agentes*, and referred to by masculine pronouns as well) have a single obligation, enforced by the threat of death: to allow the egg to take shape. The initial relation of writer to textual production, which is manifested in the exuberant verbal play and doubled in the narrative situation of a mother feeding her children, shifts into a more somber mode. Unknown and ruthless powers exact submission and service to the egg. This submission requires not the unfolding of the "I" in the gentle, identificatory, and nurturing gestures of a mother—or at least of a Good Mother—as she cares for her children, but rather an enforced compliance, a "submission to the process" (*FL* 150), as Lispector puts it in a short piece about writing, also from *The Foreign Legion*. The author loses her stability as a subject, but not through joyfully shedding the membrane of the self, as Cixous suggests. The artistic process exacts a harsh and oppressive depersonalization. "My grievance is that in their eyes [that is, the eyes of the mysterious 'they' who command the agents] I count for nothing, I am merely precious: they look after me second by second with the most complete absence of love. . . . They want me occupied and distracted by whatever means. For with my misguided attention and my solemn folly, I might obstruct that which is being made through me. The fact is, I myself, I myself strictly speaking, have only served to obstruct" (*FL* 54).

In this parable, the author is not a coherent, self-present being who gives out of plenitude, but rather a being who is divided and unknown to herself. Her art takes shape through a mysterious and harshly demanding process. The relation of "agent" to "egg" takes on an adversary edge: devotion is tainted by resentment and submission by rebellion. "There are instances of agents who commit suicide: they find the few instructions they have been given insufficient, and feel they have no support" (*FL* 53). The chicken at least knew how to bring forth and protect the egg, even if she did not know why. The commerce between the narrator as agent, the "they" who command her, and the egg becomes more conflictive. She is not certain that she is an agent or, alternatively, surmises that her betrayals of the egg might also have been mandated and foreseen:

> There is also the time which they have given me, and which they give us so that the egg may take shape in honest idleness. And I have used this time for forbidden pleasures and forbidden sorrows, completely forgetting about the egg. That is my simplicity. Or is that exactly what they want to happen to me, so that the egg may fulfill itself? Is this freedom or am I being compelled? For it is now becoming clear that every error on my part has been exploited. (*FL* 54)

In working out the disjunctions and continuities between nurture and artistic creation, Lispector—with terrible irony, with implacable wit—assigns to a female creature, the chicken, that emblem of befuddled domesticity, the role of artist. The chicken occupies this position not because of any particularly admirable feminine traits, but because of a dim-witted devotion paired with an inability to comprehend the uncontrollable process in which she participates. Artists, Lispector seems to be saying, share the chicken's devotion to shaping forms whose significance lies ultimately beyond their grasp. The metaphorical slippage from "chicken" to "agent" directs attention away from the specific qualities of female creation and traces instead the connection between the female condition, the negative capabilities that all artists possess, and, more harshly still, the dependence by all artists on unpredictable forces beyond their control.

In this story, the narrator as nurturer and the narrator as artist ultimately stand in contrast to each other. Whereas the narrator actively controls her mothering function, feeding and loving her children, as artist she plays out a more passive role. In the final paragraph of the story, she is the passive receptor of a presence whose arrival or withdrawal she cannot predict:

> Out of devotion to the egg, I forgot about it. My necessary forgetfulness. My calculating forgetfulness. For the egg is elusive. Confronted by my possessive adoration, the egg can withdraw never to return. But suppose the egg were to be forgotten. Suppose I were to make the sacrifice of only living my life and forgetting about the egg. Suppose the egg were to be impossible. Then—free, delicate, without any message for me—perhaps once more the egg might move from space right up to this window which I have always kept open. And, at dawn, it might descend into our apartment. Serenely move into the kitchen. Illuminating it with my pallor. (*FL* 55)

This is an *ars poetica* that recognizes a necessary traffic with the less kindly forces of the unconscious—a possible interpretation of the "they" who control the agents—and the need for a humiliating, perplexed submission to them. This poetics entails investments toward the text, toward the reader, and then back toward the narrating subject herself; such investments include a painful awareness of conflict, of limitations, of the ridiculous, and of an inevitable passivity toward psychic obsessions. Occasionally, these turbulent inner forces cohere—like the egg that comes in through the kitchen window—with the illuminating persuasiveness of a subtle, compelling form.

In this story, then, writing and nurturing are not twin articulations of the feminine, as Cixous would have it, but are instead irreparably disjoined. The writer who mothers does not mother when she writes, but enters a harsh realm where she struggles for mastery with powers that require her submission. In Cixous's apparently nurturing reception of Lispector, mastering and appropriative forces are also inevitably at work, as I have tried to show.[7] By positing an implicit identification between her literary concerns and Lispector's, Cixous becomes blind to elements of Lispector's text that cannot be easily assimilated to her thesis.

IV

If Cixous's approach to Lispector's text, so conscious and well intentioned, is compromised by the pressures of identification, how, then, can one perform a reading that is truly open to the alterity of the other? For a nurturing reception, modeled after an ideal mother's self-effacing attention to her child's needs, is, of course, the very opposite of a reading that assimilates, appropriates, and, by giving priority to one's own concerns, inevitably betrays. Lispector confronts a similar problem, on the level of fiction, when, in *The Hour of the Star*, she depicts the interiority of Macabéa, a poor young woman who occupies the position of other (in socioeconomic and cultural terms) relative not only to the author but also to the likely reader of the novel.[8] (This work will be discussed in greater detail in chapter 5.) Instead of using a narrator who could in some way merge with the author, or an impersonal narrator who would dilute a personal vision in anonymity, Lispector chooses to emphasize the dilemma of the approach to the other as she interposes a mediator between writer and character, the narrator, Rodrigo S. M., who dramatizes the difficulties that confront him as he attempts to write Macabéa.

This narrator, one of the more controversial aspects of the text, complicates the binary relation between author and character, blocking more direct projections and identifications. Cixous, in "The Author in Truth," writes that the masculine narrator increases the distance between author and character, making possible a respect that is uncontaminated by the pity Macabéa would inevitably evoke in a female narrator. "Macabéa needs a very special author. It is out of love for Macabéa that Clarice Lispector will create the necessary author" (AT 138). "It is as a man in extremity, as a stripped being who gives up all pleasures including football, that Clarice—no, he—finds the most respectful distance from her little slip of a woman" (AT 144). Insisting upon love and respect, Cixous ignores the other, contradictiory emotions that make up the varied repertory of the narrator: paternalism, condescension, mockery, even cruelty. Identification does not disappear, of course, but is inserted into a more ample spectrum from which not even betrayal is excluded. "Even you, Brutus?!" (Lispector 1986b, 84) the narrator asks himself during the long final scene in which he joins with the forces of fate and kills Macabéa. The project of reading without betraying that Cixous attributes to Lispector's depictions of objects and beings, and describes as the path she herself attempts to follow with the "extreme fidelity" of her critical interpretation, is a project that Lispector counters in *The Hour of the Star* with a reading that betrays, a reading conscious of its deforming specularity, as well as of its blindnesses, antipathies, and indifferences. It is this more heterogeneous reading, however, that does not censor negative emotions, that paradoxically permits the other to "remain absolutely strange within the greatest possible proximity," retaining more of the alterity that Cixous's nurturing reading of Lispector ultimately censors and disallows.

4
A Woman Writing: Fiction and Autobiography in *The Stream of Life* and *The Stations of the Body*

> *It's useless to try to define me: I simply slip away, genres can't catch me.*
>
> The Stream of Life
>
> *Frazer no extremo, onde o risco começa*
> [*Working on the edge, where risk begins*]
> João Cabral de Melo Neto

Some writers, in their maturity, bring to new levels of refinement and effectiveness the repertory of forms they developed in their earlier years. Lispector belongs to the different breed of those who end their careers by questioning the very forms they have shaped. Lispector's late narratives register an eagerness to try out new directions and, by implication, a critique of her earlier achievements. The conflicting forces that had been visible mainly in the realm of representation—her characters and their fictive worlds—now also come to govern her insistent inquiry about the value of her writing, and of literature itself, about the boundaries between fiction and autobiography, about the competing and contradictory strategies and claims of high art and popular fiction. Lispector interrogates the motives for literary production, even the moral worth of the writer's activity, as well as the nature of the reader's engagement with the literary text. Throughout this questioning, gender is always at issue. If she constantly asks herself, and the reader, in the explicit metafictional dimension of her texts, what it means to write, she also asks what it means for a woman to write. Does the woman artist, by virtue of her sex, have access to special psychic states? Does she incur special obligations of decorum and maternal concern toward characters and readers? Or is it her obligation to transgress conventional notions of respectability and prescribed gender-marked behaviors? These questions, which occupied some of Lispector's characters from her earliest fiction, now take a more urgent and, at times, aggressive tone because they apply to *this* writer, the narrator who writes the very text now in our hands.

Two instances of Lispector's late fiction, *The Stream of Life* (*Água viva*, 1973) and *The Stations of the Body* (*A via crucis do corpo*, 1974), can lead us into a closer examination of concerns that dominated the writing of her final years. Although different in many ways, both are transgressive texts. *The Stream of Life*, in its first edition subtitled "fiction," drastically curtails or eliminates the usual elements of narrative fiction. The only character is the self-reflexive narrator, a painter who meditates on art and life, addressing the reader and a shadowy former lover (addressees who seem to blur into one another). The plots are rudimentary: the protagonist's daily, routine activities; the fluctuations of her spirits from exaltation to dejection and back again; and the plots of dreams, allegorical fantasies, and vignettes, which barely form before they dissipate. In contrast, the stories of *The Stations of the Body* almost reduce themselves to character and plot—bluntly drawn, stereotypical characters, in many cases, and plots about sex and violence—interspersed with wry, distancing comments from the narrator. This collection baffled Lispector's readers, who were accustomed to her dense web of introspective meditations. Not surprisingly, the contemporary reviews were mostly negative; one bears the title "Yes, It's Trash" (Becherucci 1974). We have, then, two opposite extremes: in *The Stream of Life*, "a monologue with life" (the subtitle of an earlier draft of the book), devoid of the usual underpinnings of fictional characters and circumstances; in *The Stations of the Body*, a reckless plunge into catchy plots and characters.

Yet these two texts also share important elements. *The Stations of the Body* contains four short autobiographical narratives, in which, as in *The Stream of Life*, the woman who writes discusses her own writing. In both texts, certain circumstances of the narrator's life coincide with Lispector's, and the female writing persona oscillates in power, shifting from grandiose claims of contact with the essence of reality to plaintive recognition of diminishment and failure. As a way into these difficult texts, I will attempt to define the writing personae and to interpret the intersections of autobiography and fiction. In broader terms, these two texts will serve as examples of the turbulences and the pressing against formal limits that came to mark Lispector's late fiction.

I

Early in *The Stream of Life* the protagonist announces: "There are many things I can't tell you. I'm not going to be autobiographical. I want to be 'bio.' I write as the words flow" (*SL* 26).[1] A diffidence with regard to the "auto" and the "graphical" marks this text, which nevertheless hinges on meditations about the inner life and writing of a first-person narrator. Suspicion about "writing oneself" is manifested by the erasure of particularizing traits. The nameless narrator offers us few clues to her personal circumstances: she is a woman (her gender is foregrounded) living in the company of a maid in an apartment overlooking the sea. The reduction of personal facts to a minimum (still bearing, nevertheless, the marks of class and privilege) seems motivated by the hope of achieving broad representation: "And if I say 'I,' it's because I don't dare say 'you,' or 'we,' or 'a person.' I am limited to the humble act of self-personalization through reducing myself, but I am the 'you-are' " (*SL* 6). The depersonalization is also, then, a suprapersonalization, a wish to represent not a self within its narrow boundaries, but what it has in common (or fantasizes it has in common) with living creatures and even living matter: "I want to be 'bio.' "

Writing itself also comes under suspicion: it appears as a treacherous medium to the narrator, who yearns to convey the realm "behind thinking." Here, as often occurs in Lispector, the danger of words lies in their allegiance to the already codified, to logic and the rational intelligence. Words may be necessary instruments but might best be used "like bait":

> a word fishing for what is not a word. When that non-word—the whatever's between the lines—bites the bait, something has been written. Once the between the lines has been hooked, you can throw the word away with relief. (*SL* 14)

As in the fishing metaphor, a desire to plumb depths persists: "I'm writing you as if I were tearing the snarled roots of a colossal tree from the depths of the earth" (*SL* 13). The persona of the painter-who-writes, only recently turning to the medium of words, also figures the will to escape the already codified and the constructions of the rational intelligence. "I want to write you as someone who is learning" (*SL* 8), the narrator says. "My writing is coarse and disorderly" (*SL* 4). It is as if her very clumsiness with words could facilitate her grasp of what lies beyond words: "I want for myself the vibrant substratum of words" (*SL* 5).

There are no internal divisions in the novella, except for the double-spaced blanks that divide the paragraphs from each other (in the Portuguese text, not in the English translation), connecting them loosely in paratactic juxtaposition. The preference for a verbal improvisation, so often invoked, signals the desire to elude both the strictures of any preconceived form and, as in the free association of psychoanalysis, the dead grip of the conscious mind. "I know what I'm doing here . . . I'm improvising. But what's wrong with that? I improvise in the same way they improvise in jazz, frenzied jazz, I improvise in front of an audience" (*SL* 15).

We should take note of the reference to an audience. This improvisation, this writing what comes to mind, should not be confused with Lispector's method of composition, and certainly should not be taken as her only method. In *The Stream of Life*, the complexly inscribed subject refuses autobiography and stages its conflicts with both "auto" and "graphical." She regards with suspicion the writing of the self, yet also refuses to confine herself to the repertory of fictional techniques: character, plot, setting. The result is a borderline, hybrid text that thwarts compartmentalization, as the narrator is well aware: "It is useless to try to classify me: I simply slip away, genres can't catch me" (*SL* 7). It is worth examining the autobiographical origins and encroachments of this text before attempting to define the (if only thinly) fictionalized persona whose grand ambition is nothing less than being the observing receptor of the flow of life: "This is life seen by life. I may not make sense but it's the same lack of sense of a throbbing vein" (*SL* 8).

It is possible to examine Lispector's discarded choices for *The Stream of Life*, including the initial choice of an autobiographical protagonist, in an early, undated draft, entitled "Objeto gritante" ("Screaming Object").[2] One of only two complete typescripts of Lispector's novels or collections of stories available in public archives [3] (other manuscripts are believed to be held privately by her family and cannot easily be consulted), this 188-page (legal-size) typescript is a complete early version of *The Stream of Life*. It already bears the new title, *Água viva*, parenthetically on the title page, written in Lispector's large, diagonal script. Many corrections are made in ink throughout the manuscript, also in Lispector's hand.[4]

"Screaming Object" (a title she fortunately discarded) offers, among its wealth of material for study, a glimpse of Lispector's process of composition that counters widely held notions that her creative method was largely improvisatory, notions sustained by her commentators, her writer-characters, and sometimes by Lispector herself in interviews. It is clear, as Benedito Nunes points out, that Lispector was "willfully careless about the preservation of originals" (so few are left) and about "the correction of her texts once they were in print" (Nunes 1988, xxxv). It is also likely, as Nunes believes and Lispector herself affirms on many occasions, that

> the involvement in writing came before the idea, because the idea was discovered by her through its verbal expression, which guided her thought, as if a torrent of phrases were dictated through her. . . . Fragments constituted, then, the basic elements of the narrative in progress. In other words, the elaboration of the narrative, in the intermittent rhythm of

writing, finds in the fragment its first and decisive moment. (Nunes 1988, xxxv)

What is not borne out in the examination of "Screaming Object" is the notion that Lispector did not rewrite or significantly alter her text once she put it down on paper. Benedito Nunes supposes that "the variants would not bring substantial alteration to the preliminary text, which would be much more than a simple outline or draft" (Nunes 1988, xxxvi). However, when we compare the early draft of *The Stream of Life* with the published version we find changes that range from substitutions, additions, and deletions of words and sentences, to drastic cuts or additions of larger fragments, to shifts in subjects of certain anecdotes (from "he" or "she" to "I," for instance). We also discover the major alteration that guided many of the local changes and that is the focus of my comments: Lispector's erasure of the autobiographical persona used in the early draft.

Although Lispector already ostensibly rejects autobiography ("This is simple because it is not autobiography. It is pure thinking-feeling"),[5] an unmistakably autobiographical first person dominates the text. She is a writer and a mother who has traveled widely in Europe and recounts incidents of her life, including references to a serious burn (Lispector was burned in a fire in 1967). I do not mean to imply that the autobiographical persona is the "true" Lispector, presenting an unvarnished version of her life, but, rather, that in assuming that persona, she incurs the conventions of another genre. As she corrected this draft, she seems to have had second thoughts about the writer-protagonist: midway through this early version she begins to replace "writing" with "painting" (and less often with "speaking") and "writer" with "painter." The more elaborate painter persona is not yet in evidence. The narrator in the early draft is continuous with the autobiographical "I" Lispector had been developing in the weekly columns or *crônicas* that she wrote for the *Jornal do Brasil* from 1967 to 1973, the year that *The Stream of Life* was published. Many sections of the early drafts reproduce those *crônicas*, and the new passages continue the conversational style of casual personal reference. The layers of autobiography and self-quotation, however, reach further into the past. Here it would be relevant to make an excursus into Lispector's reprinting of previous writings.

In her newspaper *crônicas* Lispector reprinted, sometimes with slight revisions, almost all of her collection of short stories, *The Foreign Legion* (*A legião estrangeira*, 1964). She explains this decision casually in a letter to her son, dated February 2, 1969: "The 'crônicas' for the *Jornal do Brasil* don't worry me because I have a bunch of them, all I have to do is choose one and there it is. Besides, I plan to 'plagiarize' myself, to publish things from *The Foreign Legion*, a book that was almost unsold because it came out at the same time as the novel [*The Passion according to G.H.*, 1964], which they preferred" (letter to Paulo Gurgel Valente, Clarice Lispector Archive). She reprinted as *crônicas* the stories (the longer ones in installments), disregarding the usual generic distinctions between the formal and fictional short story and the casual and personal *crônica*. She reprinted almost all the pieces from the section entitled "Bottom Drawer," a heterogeneous mix of aphorisms, meditations on writing, art criticism, sketches, incipient stories, and autobiographical anecdotes. It is this section, again almost complete, that made a reappearance in "Objeto gritante." It includes some of Lispector's best-known pieces, such as the analogy between writing and fishing quoted above. Some five pages of this section of the *The Foreign Legion* remain in *The Stream of Life*, as do some thirteen pages that appeared for the first time in the newspaper. Nádia Battella Gotlib dates what she terms Lispector's "circulation of texts" from the mid-1960s:

> the beginning of a period of movement of Lispector's texts among various of her publications in newspapers, magazines, and books: these texts circulate, appear and reappear, at times without any alteration, effecting a veritable ring-around-the-rosy of texts. . . . Indeed, not only do the fragments circulate, but also the characters. And Clarice herself, as Clarice, identifying herself explicitly as writer-narrator-chronicler. (Gotlib 1988, 189)

These textual reappearances contribute to the blurring of autobiography and fiction in *The Stream of Life*. Texts that were first seen in *The Foreign Legion* and in the newspaper, and that were then assimilated into the unpublished "Screaming Object" in order to define the autobiographical persona, "Clarice herself," reappear in *The Stream of Life* stripped of their autobiographical reference. For the reader familiar with Lispector's work, the effect of this textual déjà vu works against the grain of Lispector's revisions, endowing the nonautobiographical protagonist with an equivocal autobiographical resonance.

The autobiographical incursions that mark Lispector's late fiction were no doubt related to her weekly production of a *crônica* for the *Jornal do Brasil* from 1967 to 1973.[6] A free-form genre, prevalent in Brazil since the mid-nineteenth century, the *crônica* consists of a fixed newspaper space that can be filled in a variety of ways, most often with personal commentaries on current events, the arts, and the mundane or metaphysical dimensions of daily life. Some of its most famous and effective practitioners have been writers devoted to other genres, such as José de Alencar and Machado de Assis in the nineteenth century and Lispector's close contemporaries, the poets Manuel Bandeira and Carlos Drummond de Andrade. For Lispector, as no doubt for others, her weekly *crônicas* were primarily a means of earning money, and she produced them with some detachment, but they can be shown to have had a profound influence in the development of her fiction. The genre requires the creation of an autobiographical persona and the sustained reflection on communication with a wider spectrum of readers. It can, as it did for Lispector, elicit a variety of responses from her readers, in the form of letters, phone calls, and even presents, responses she wove into other *crônicas*.

During those years, Lispector was also much in demand for another autobiographical genre, the interview, despite her well-known mercurial moods, ranging from genial friendliness to a somber refusal to answer many of the questions. In the late 1960s, Lispector had practiced this genre, which attempts to link "life" and "work," also from the other side, as the interviewer of Brazilian intellectuals and other culturally prominent figures for the weekly *Manchete*. A selection of these interviews was later published as a book, *De corpo inteiro* (1975). Lispector occupied the position of a celebrated writer in Rio (and all of Brazil) during the late 1960s and 1970s with an ambivalence she frequently discussed. She was gratified but also impatient at being constricted by the role of literary figure, concerned about her privacy and the proliferation of her "real" and "false" images. Although these ambivalences are themselves *topoi* of the *crônica*, voiced by other writers, in Lispector they entered the world of her fiction, which would henceforth always include a problematic yet persistent play with autobiographical reference.

It seems likely that Lispector first planned to use autobiography in *The Stream of Life* as a sort of counterfiction, a repositioning of her obsessive themes, not in terms of invented characters, but rather in terms of "Clarice herself": a corrosive antiliterature ("This is an anti-book," she wrote on the title page of "Objeto gritante"), a "letter-book" (*livro-carta*, a term used throughout the draft). One of the four epigraphs to the draft is a phrase of Roland Barthes's: "There is no art that does not point its finger at its mask." Despite this epigraph, the early draft signals a bold attempt to remove the mask while recognizing the impossibility—and undesirability—of taking it off entirely. Lispector shows the writer *en déshabillé*—often literally dressed in a robe, with cup of coffee and cigarette in hand, in the early hours before dawn, Lispector's favorite time for writing and thinking. Yet, on the next-to-last page of *The Stream of Life*, in a passage retained from the early draft, she confesses the need for the confinement and protection of conventions: "You can't walk around naked, either in body or in spirit" (*SL* 78). In her revisions from early draft to printed fiction, she drastically reduces the elaborate staging of a woman writer "walking around naked."

We will, of course, never know all the factors that motivated Lispector's substantial revisions. Like most writers, she may have been swayed by the response of friends who read the early draft. One such response is a kind and acute letter from José Américo Pessanha, a writer and professor of philosophy who had earlier written a favorable review of *The Passion according to G.H.* (Pessanha 1976). Intellectuals such as Pessanha figured prominently in Lispector's life, both as friends and as characters in her fiction, the conflictively loved and hated *professores* of numerous Lispector texts. Many passages in Pessanha's typed letter, dated March 5, 1972, are underlined in ink, presumably by Lispector, as it originally belonged to her personal archive. Gentle and carefully worded, the letter seems a well-meaning response from someone who does not approve of the direction Lispector's work is taking, yet recognizes her need to follow her own path. After warning her that he feels unable to reach any definitive opinion, he continues:

> I tried to place the book: notes? thoughts? autobiographical fragments? I came to the conclusion that it is all of that together. . . . <u>I had the impression that you wanted to write spontaneously, a-literarily.</u> Is that so? It seems that after refusing the artifices and tricks of reason (or better yet of rationalizations) <u>you seem to want to reject the artifices of art. And to denude yourself, disguising yourself less in your own eyes and in those of the reader.</u> Hence the openness with which you show your daily mental and circumstantial life, without avoiding the juxtaposition of fragments of differing rhetorical levels and unafraid of the trivial. (Clarice Lispector Archive, Lispector's emphasis)

Pessanha attempts some practical advice, recognizing that publication may be a risk, but one worth taking. He suggests that to avoid "false appraisals" Lispector should clarify in a subtitle that the book is not intended as fiction. Although Lispector does not take this advice—instead, she categorically subtitles the final version "fiction"—she alters the text so that the subtitle becomes appropriate. She eliminates the main traces of the autobiographical process that Pessanha describes with misgivings: "Now literature comes to you and remains (or appears) immanent to your daily life: you are your own theme—as on a psychiatrist's couch where one speaks and speaks <u>without a previously rehearsed text</u>" (Clarice Lispector Archive, Lispector's emphasis). Pessanha wonders what will come next in Lispector's work, "after this meeting of you-Clarice with you-the writer": "Will you continue to be your own theme, a directly presented, naked face without the mask of character? Or will you once again speak of yourself through other voices, multiplying your mystery and your perplexity in the mirror play of character?" (Clarice Lispector Archive). Pessanha's unspoken preference for the latter option stands out clearly. In her revisions, Lispector follows his tactfully implicit advice.

Before making her revisions, however, Lispector wavers about when, and even if, to publish the book. In an interview of March 6, 1972 (the day after the date on Pessanha's letter), she said: "The book is ready, yes, but I think I will publish it only next year. . . . 'Objeto gritante' is a book that will bring on much negative criticism" (Lamare 1972; Varin 1987, 181). In another interview four and a half months later, in response to a question about this book, she states decisively: "The book will not be published. It has not achieved its goal. A writer knows when he should or shouldn't publish one of his works" (Varin 1987, 187).

Yet she did, of course, publish it the following year, in 1973. In addition to eliminating the autobiographical persona, Lispector made the text more concise (the draft, at 188 pages, is roughly double the 89 pages of the published novella) and placed a greater emphasis on moments of exaltation. In *The Stream of Life*, Lispector stages a metafictional discussion of a basic motif and subject of her writing: epiphanic moments of ecstatic, visionary insight. She eliminates plot and reduces sustained characterization to a single figure, an authorial surrogate, the writer-painter.

We might profitably describe the heights of empowerment of the first-person narrator in terms of the "female sublime." Patricia Yaeger argues that "in recent decades, women have begun to write in the sublime mode—a mode which has conventionally been the domain of masculine writers and poets. Its most conspicuous practitioners are those writers we have labelled 'French Feminists'" (Yaeger 1989, 191). Yaeger believes that Irigaray and Cixous, despite their differences, engage in a common project: "to reinvent the sublime as a feminine mode—to invent for women a vocabulary of ecstasy and empowerment, a new way of reading feminine experience" (Yaeger 1989, 1920). Yaeger charts several varieties of the female sublime, finding instances of it in such diverse writers as Elizabeth Bishop, Eudora Welty, and Nikki Giovanni. I would suggest that the quest for a female sublime shapes several of Lispector's texts, and perhaps none as insistently as *The Stream of Life*. In Lispector's hands, this mode does not follow exactly any of the three patterns Yaeger identifies as "three strategies the woman writer uses to harness and re-invent a sublimating power that has been too exclusively associated with male writers" ("the failed sublime," "the sovereign sublime," and the "feminine or pre-oedipal sublime" (Yaeger 1989, 199-205). Yaeger's discussion is, nevertheless, suggestive and helpful in identifying Lispector's particular strategies.

"The claim of the sublime is that we can—in words or feelings—transcend the normative, the human," Yaeger affirms (1989, 192). We find a yearning for that transcendence throughout the novella, a text pitched at an intense emotional level, beginning with a cry of mingled joy and pain:

> It's with such intense joy. It's such an hallelujah. "Hallelujah," I shout, an hallelujah that fuses with the darkest human howl of the pain of separation but is a shout of diabolical happiness. Because nobody holds me back anymore. (*SL* 3)

This specifically female power the protagonist assumes—hence the appropriateness of the term "female sublime"—derives first from the nurture of a maternal presence, as revealed in the words following the above quotation: "I still have the ability to reason—I've studied mathematics, which is the madness of reason—but now I want plasma, I want to feed directly from the placenta" (*SL* 3).

The image of feeding from the placenta varies in each of its five occurrences in the book. First, the "I" draws surprising strength from the position of an unborn infant, the most dependent of human beings. Oneness with the mother, pre-birth and certainly pre-Oedipal, displaces the rule of reason and provides an alternate source of power. In its second appearance, however, the image becomes a curious kind of female self-mothering: "I am told that after a cat gives birth it eats its own placenta and for four days doesn't eat anything more. Only after that will it drink milk" (*SL* 22). This solipsistic nourishment, a nondamaging self-devouring, possible only for the female who has just given birth, recurs several times. Eating the placenta comes to represent the self-sustaining stamina for further artistic quests that the artist draws from her own productivity: "I am not lying. My truth sparkles like the prism of a crystal chandelier. But it is hidden. I can stand it because I am strong: I've eaten my own placenta" (*SL* 34-35).

The impetus toward transcendence in the novella needs to be constantly reasserted because it is part of a dizzying roller-coaster effect that alternates between exaltation and dejection. The narrator experiences a number of symbolic births and deaths, told, as is the rest of the text, in the present tense ("Marvellous scandal. I am born" [*SL* 27]; then, a few pages later, "I'm about to die and form new compositions" [*SL* 31]). Moments of insight, of joy, dissipate and then regain momentum. The quest may be frustrated ("I am Diana, the Huntress of gold, and I find only boneyards" [*SL* 18]) or an initially arresting revelation may prove empty: "I don't think, just as the diamond doesn't think. I shine, totally clear. I have two eyes that are open. Open to nothing. To the ceiling" (*SL* 32). The oscillation between exaltation and dejection follows no discernibly logical pattern, but is simply a rhythmic alternation like the in and out of breathing (a physiological process that the narrator often invokes). The "deaths" and "rebirths" depend on each other, recurring in cycles: "Will I have to die again in order to be reborn again? I accept" (*SL* 35).

Any attempt to interpret these reversals of power should take into account the novella's specific structure of address. The "I" speaks to a "you," a former lover whom she invokes sporadically throughout the text, addressee of her barbed words. One of the narrator's "rebirths" results from the lovers' separation:

> I come from long suffering, I come from the hell of love, but now I am free of you. I come from far away—from a weighty ancestry. . . . And crazily I latch onto the corners of myself, my hallucinations suffocate me with their beauty. I am before, I am almost, I am never. And all this I gained when I stopped loving you. (*SL* 10-11)

This lover, whose departure makes possible such an exhilarating absence of limits, is not an entirely stable addressee. At times the narrator admits that she only pretends to write to "you," or that what she writes he would not care to read: "You'll never read what I write. And when I've recorded my secret of being—I'll throw it away as if into the sea" (*SL* 60). Yet, as imagined addressee, he represents an antagonist crucial to her writing: he must be won over, or dismissed, but he cannot be ignored. The addressee's masculine gender is made explicit only once in the text, but then unequivocally: "Eu te conheço todo por te viver toda'" (my emphasis), a generic specificity that is lost in the English translation: "I know you through and through by having lived you completely" (*SL* 42). He represents the allegiance to rationality shared by many other masculine figures, lovers-antagonists, in Lispector's fiction. "You, who are in the habit of wanting to know why" (*SL* 5) is offered a text that rejects the rules of logic: "Could it be that what I'm writing you is behind thinking? What it definitely is not is rationality. Anyone who can stop reasoning—which is a terribly difficult thing to do—should come with me" (*SL* 24). Yet the need somehow to reach, appease, or seduce this addressee remains: "I write to you because you don't quite accept what I am" (*SL* 60). "But I want to have the freedom of saying things without connection as a profound way of reaching you" (*SL* 68). "To write you I first cover myself with perfume" (*SL* 42).

The narrator's revelations, then, are directed to a resistant or indifferent addressee, who must be pulled into and made to accept this oscillating, contradictory discourse based on collapsible dichotomies and juxtaposed statements that refute one another. The interpellations to the "you," present on almost every page, become also an address to the reader. They form an insistent web of cajolery, challenge, accusation, or even pathetic pleading: "God help me, I'm lost. I need you terribly. We have to be two. So that the wheat can be tall" (*SL* 32). The ambivalent relation with the narratee shifts vertiginously in terms of connection, separation, and relative power. Metaphors of birth underline mutual gifts and needs implied in the textual exchange: "I'm giving you freedom. First, I break the water sac. Then, I cut the umbilical cord. And you are alive, on your own" (*SL* 26). On the next page, the roles are reversed: "You who read me, help me to be born" (*SL* 27).

At once lover, reader, and fragment of a divided subjectivity, the "you" figures the resistant space toward which the narrator directs her words and from which she must wrest validation for a writing that, as in so many modern and postmodern texts, disregards the constraints of genre, of basic narrative structures, of logical progression and coherence. That validation, although strenuously sought, never comes. In the next to last paragraph of the novella, Lispector continues to imagine a writing that finds no welcoming reception. The pact between writer and reader inscribed in this text is a tenuous and difficult encounter between two narcissisms that merge and separate without quite recognizing each other. "Look at me and love me. No: you look at yourself and love yourself. That's what's right" (*SL* 79).

The escape from the constraints of traditional literary forms is also, of course, an escape from the Oedipal patterns of narrative: the strictures of active male subjects and passive female objects. Only traces of these strictures remain in the need to posit a writing directed against another order and in the enthusiastic courting of freedom and excess. "I know no limits. And my own strength frees me, that full life that overflows within me. And I plan nothing in the intuitive labor that is my living: I labor with the indirect, the informal and the unforeseen" (*SL* 31). The break with the male lover, and with the rule of reason posited as masculine, goes along with a celebration of female specificities. The Whitmanesque boast of the "I" 's capaciousness is tinged with gender and sex-linked characteristics: "But when winter comes I give and give and give. I shelter and cradle broods of people to my warm breast" (*SL* 51). "The excess of me starts to hurt and when I'm excessive I have to give of myself, like the milk that if it doesn't flow engorges the breast" (*SL* 65).

The narrator who seeks to deny or transcend the limits of genres, of literature itself ("This isn't a book because this isn't how one should write" [*SL* 6]; "What I'm writing you is not for you to read, it's for you to be" [*SL* 28]), also stretches the limits of individual identity, moving from depersonalization to suprapersonalization and even to the claim that these two states coincide: "I surpass myself, abdicating my name, and then I am the world" (*SL* 49). "Behind my own thought is the truth that is the world's" (*SL* 70). Yet also exhilarating are the moments of exact self-possession: "In this territory of being what one is, I am pure crystalline ecstasy. One is. I am myself. You are yourself" (*SL* 21). Another move of this elastic "I" is the identification with the subhuman animal world, as well as with a world of imagined (perhaps stereotypically imagined) fantastic beings, a night world of transgressive rites—even bloody, orgiastic ones—where she embraces with eagerness what conventional morality shuns:

> But I know still another life. I know and want it and I devour it ferociously. It's a life of magic violence. It's mysterious and bewitching. In it snakes coil around each other while the stars tremble. Drops of water fall in the phosphorescent darkness of the cave. In this darkness the flowers grow entangled in an enchanted and moist garden. And I am the sorceress of this mute bacchanal. (*SL* 57)

The "female sublime" aspects of the novella may indeed put some readers off as self-indulgent and solipsistic: cries of vulnerability alternate with a haughty superiority, a version of the *hypsos*, or height, of the traditional sublime (Yaeger 1989, 194) that is associated with prerogatives linked to female biology or gender. There is a gratuitous quality to the power that suddenly invests the narrator and then, equally mysteriously, vanishes. For these reasons the novella is not, to my mind, an entirely successful work. It is, however, an adventurous, even reckless, attempt to tune into and flaunt alternative sources of creative power: the mystical (although not the religious), the intuitive, the magical. In its elaborate staging of a creative process that is antirational and, as such, posited as antimasculine, the novella offers an intense depiction of a subjectivity battling with conflicting forces and an interiority attempting to come to terms with the depletions of time, solitude, and death, as well as with moments of overwhelming persuasion that she is in contact with exalting forces unavailable to common mortals. The autobiographical origins of *The Stream of Life* suggest that the novella describes the psychic dynamics that propelled Lispector's writing and the reception she imagines for it. It contains a diffident, self-doubting, but at the same time audacious, challenge to literary conventions and a vindication of a different sort of writing. A narrowly autobiographical reading of the novella is surely inadequate, but an awareness of autobiographical elements allows us to recognize both its fictional components and its representation of the psychic oscillations that drive Lispector's imagination.

II

In *The Stations of the Body*, the autobiographical first person continues as a focus for metafictional reflection. "Clarice herself" considers an expanding set of issues that includes the relation between fiction, the brutal facts of social life, and the delicate, compromised position of "the famous woman writer" who purveys a fiction that deals in sex and violence. This collection brings together two diametrically opposed sorts of narratives: fictional stories, written on commission and marked by an ironic sensationalism, and autobiographical narratives that discuss those uneasy incursions into commercial fiction. How can we interpret the juxtaposition of the fictional stories and the autobiographical ones? What is the relation between the "I" who narrates—a woman ("Clarice herself") concerned with matters of propriety, leading a life of measured sociability and carefully conducted affections—and the many fictional selves she creates, slightly ridiculous or distinctly disreputable characters who pursue sex out of love, lust, hate, or financial gain? The surprising juxtaposition of the two narrative modes suggests these questions, and we might look for answers in the play of echoes and shadows between the autobiographical and the fictional stories.[7]

In *The Stations of the Body* a transgressive sexuality is brought to the fore by insistent repetition, variation, and metafictional reflection. The fictional stories feature plots about adultery, homosexuality, bisexuality, the sexual desire of spinsters and old women, of a nun and a priest, as well as about varieties of sexual crime (rape and jealousy-motivated murder) and sex for sale (prostitution, transvestism, a boy lover kept by an old woman). All of them challenge, most of them successfully, the patriarchal authority that has repressed the sexuality of women. As we will see in "Pig Latin" (discussed in chapter 5), these stories have a farcical dimension and stress plot and dialogue instead of the complex interior processes of Lispector's earlier stories. They enact literally the violence previously restricted to the figurative language used to describe the characters' inner lives.

Despite their simple syntax and occasional vulgar words, the stories are hardly titillating. The sexual incidents, far from being graphic or sensual, tend toward the sad, the vengeful, the humiliating, and the comic. The sensational plots of some of the stories—the English spinster seduced by an extraterrestrial in "Miss Algrave," the replay of the virgin birth in "The Way of the Cross," and the bigamist murdered by his two lesbian companions in "The Body"—suggest a parodic version of stories carried under eye-catching headlines in sensational newspapers. The reliance on stock characters and dramatic turning points is the mark of another pop culture genre, the soap opera, which in Brazil attracts vast primetime audiences.[8] We have, then, a "debased" fiction, contaminated by the narrative commonplaces of a commercialized popular culture, that ironically celebrates the overturning of the law, in most cases signaling the victory of women over patriarchal law: crimes without punishment and the lifting of sexual repressions. The police are ineffective or lax in these stories, as are their counterparts who regulate literary and sexual propriety. At the end of "The Body," the two investigating policemen, faced with irrefutable evidence of the murder and the guilt of the two women, prefer to ignore it:

> "Look," said one of the policemen, right in front of the astonished secretary, "it's best to pretend that nothing at all happened, otherwise there will be a lot of noise, lots of paperwork, lots of gossip."
> "You two," said the other policeman, "pack your bags and go and live in Montevideo. And don't bother us any more." (*SB* 23-24)[9]

In the autobiographical stories, Lispector reflects on her own transgressions against a devotion to "serious" literature that her readers and critics had come to expect and her possibly compromising involvement with fiction on sexual themes, aimed at a broader public. Lispector's misgivings about the value of literature are evident in many ways. The autobiographical narrator is impatient with the cult of other writers and even of her own image and work. In "For the Time Being" she claims not to have a single book by Machado de Assis in her house and to forget whether she ever even read José de Alencar (the two most important Brazilian novelists of the nineteenth century). In 'Day by Day" she thinks, in response to a friend's warning about the risk of writing a pornographic book: "Who knows if this book will add anything to my works? Damn my works. I don't know why people attach so much importance to literature. As for my name? To hell with it, I've got other things to think about" (*SB* 44).

In the fictional stories, the devaluation of serious literature is not discussed, but enacted: the stories stress bluntly told and emphatic actions rather than refinements of feeling and thought. We might think of some of the stories as parodies of Lispector's earlier fiction. "Miss Algrave," for instance, built around an epiphanic encounter, follows a pattern that Lispector had used in her short stories of the early 1960s (*Family Ties*, 1960; *The Foreign Legion*, 1964). In those works, the many encounters—with a blind man, with a powerful yet emotionally afflicted old man, with a buffalo, or with a bunch of tiny roses—put the protagonists in touch with waves of contradictory feelings and opened vistas into morally turbulent worlds, represented in Lispector's finely tuned language of oxymora and antitheses. In "Miss Algrave," the encounter is sexual and takes place with an extraterrestrial, who enters her room through the open window. The epiphany is the sexual union itself, bringing with it no inexpressible complexities: "She had never felt what she felt. It was too good. She was afraid that it might end. It was as if a cripple had thrown his cane into the air" (*SB* 11). This patriarch from outer space, wearing a crown of interlaced snakes and a purple cape, orders her rudely about, but nevertheless helps her overcome her submission to the male rule on earth. Miss Algrave's repressions are magically lifted, she finds pleasure and profit in prostitution, and even plans, with vengeful glee, to become her boss's mistress. I would suggest that Lispector shows a similar glee in embracing the stereotypical simplicities and sensational bluntness of this very different narrative style, mocking for the moment her own more subtle and labored literary achievements. The parodic aspect of *The Stations of the Body*, then, cuts two ways: against sensational fiction, whose strategies Lispector uses and mocks, and against her earlier narratives, structured around "serious" epiphanies. As in "A Chicken" and "The Smallest Woman in the World" in *Family Ties*, Lispector is her own sharp critic, transposing recognizable ingredients of her earlier stories into a parodic register.

The subtlety and complexity of *The Stations of the Body* lie mainly in the interaction between the various short texts and in the questions suggested by their juxtaposition, especially in the concerns of the autobiographical narratives when seen against the unfolding of the fictional stories. In the three-page "Explanation" that opens the collection, Lispector addresses two main questions that are crucial not only to the fictional stories, but also to all her later narratives: the relation of the fictive imagination to the violence of social life and the degree to which a writer's invention of characters is either mimetic of social reality or self-expressive (issues that, as we will see, loom large in *The Hour of the Star*). Lispector, uneasy about possible accusations of commercialism, of the prostitution, as it were, of her art, launches into multiple, ironic, and contradictory explanations. Her editor commissioned her "to write three stories which, said he, had really happened.... And the subject was dangerous":

> I told him that I didn't know how to write commissioned stories. But—
> even as he talked to me over the phone—I began to feel inspiration
> growing in me. The phone conversation was on Friday. I began on

Saturday. Sunday morning the three stories were ready: "Miss Algrave," "The Body" and "The Way of the Cross." All the stories in this book are bruising stories. And I was the one who suffered most. If there are indecencies in these stories, the fault is not mine. It's useless to say they didn't happen to me, my own family and my friends. How do I know? I know. Artists know things. I just want to tell you that I don't write for money but rather on impulse. They will throw stones at me. It hardly matters. I'm not playing games, I'm an honorable woman. Besides, it was a challenge. (*SB* 3)

Lispector disclaims responsiblility for the violent and sexual goings-on of her stories by blaming them on her editor's request and also on the mimesis of her fiction: the waywardness of the world is responsible for her unchaste and violent plots. She seeks further relief from the vertigo of sexuality (or commercialism) by offering to write under a pseudonym, but the editor refuses:

He said that I ought to have the freedom to write whatever I wanted to. What could I do but be my own victim? I just pray to God no one ever commissions anything from me again. For it looks like I'm likely to rebelliously obey, I the unliberated one. (*SB* 3-4)

One can guess at the marketing strategies that might have led her editor to dream of combining Lispector's critical success as a writer of serious fiction with the sales potential of stories about sex, designs her use of a pseudonym would surely disrupt. Several well-known Brazilian writers—Nelson Rodrigues, Dalton Trevisan, and Rubem Fonseca—had, in the 1950s and 1960s, produced successful and literarily inventive short fiction that was extremely compressed—often into just a few pages of succinct sexual and/or violent encounters. Their stories claimed, in ironic and colloquial language, to represent the commonplace scandals of reality: "Life As It Really Is" is the title of Nelson Rodrigues's two-volume collection of short stories (1961). Their narratives are, in different ways, hybrids of literary and popular fiction. Lispector's editor might have thought to steer her in a similar direction, seeing the turn her fiction had been taking. *Where You Were at Night* (*Onde estivestes de noite*, 1974), published a few months before *The Stations of the Body*, contains similar stories about sex. The two collections even have a story in common, "A Complicated Case" (the English translation avoids this repetition), a story that had been published earlier as a *crônica* in the *Jornal do Brasil* (February 3, 1973; Lispector 1992, 593-95) with the title "An Anecdote Worthy of Nelson Rodrigues." In it Lispector repeats the intertextual references to the mode of short fiction she is considering and parodying: "It would take a writer like Dalton Trevisan to unravel the plot," and later, "I am as refined as Nelson Rodrigues, who does not neglect cruel details" (Lispector 1992, 593-94).[10] The new mode of Lispector's fiction is not, then, simply a response to someone else's suggestion, but is the result of an internal, as much as an external, demand.

Nelson Rodrigues, Dalton Trevisan, and Rubem Fonseca were notorious for their violent, sexually explicit, and staunchly *machista* fiction. Using them as models whom Lispector ambivalently emulates and counters in *The Stations of the Body* was not without problems for a woman writer. A central issue—compliance with the rules of sexual respectability—is played out in contrasting ways in the autobiographical and in the fictional stories: whereas the autobiographical narrator protests (ironically) her obedience to patriarchal notions of propriety, the fictional characters brazenly flaunt them, setting up a curious play of contrasts and oppositions between fiction and autobiography.

The first person in these stories is situated much like Lispector: a famous writer, divorced, the mother of two sons, doting owner of a little dog, and so forth. She presents herself as an ordinary woman, concerned with the mundane matters of everyday living. She comments on solitude, death, and the ebb and flow of psychic energy, dwelling particularly on moments of despondence, when the will to live seems to grind to a halt. This first person, occupied with thinking over in somewhat rambling fashion the day-to-day matters of living and writing, contrasts with the characters in the fictional stories, whose activities are dramatic and purposeful (if often mischievous), thereby firmly distinguishing between the ruminations of a respectable writer and the lawless behavior of her characters.

The autobiographical narrator's stress on respectability is bolstered by insistent references to Mother's Day. She claims to have written some of her more outrageous stories on Mother's Day, the date of the autobiographical narratives as well. "Today is the 12th of May, Mother's Day. It wouldn't make sense to write stories on this day that I wouldn't want my children to read because I'd be ashamed" (*SB* 3). Two other autobiographical narratives are written on Mother's Day, the last on May 13, celebrated as the day of abolition in Brazil, "the day of freedom for the slaves—therefore for me, too" (*SB* 4). Mother's Day becomes the focus for a complicated and ironic consideration of a woman writer's freedom from or obedience to the rules of propriety, and of whether her nature is respectably moral and maternal or whether it renders her vulnerable to the seductions of commercialism and adventurous sexual fantasies.

For the autobiographical narrator, motherhood is a bedrock value and a role she leans on for support. In "Day After Day," she answers a friend's warning against writing a pornographic book by assuming the position of a dutiful mother, obedient to patriarchal authority: "I've already asked my son's permission, I said he shouldn't read my book. And I told him a bit about the stories I've written. He listened and said: that's O.K." (*SB* 44). Even the dominant carnal desires of this narrator are motherly desires: "I'm full of yearning," she confesses in "For the Time Being." "Yearning for my children, yes, flesh of my flesh. Weak flesh and I haven't read all the books. La chair est triste" (*SB* 42).

In "The Man Who Appeared," assuming the role of the mother separates and protects the autobiographical narrator from the unwise sexual liaisons of many of her fictional characters. The narrator encounters a drunk in the street and, recognizing him despite his ravaged appearance, extends a hardly prudent invitation: " 'Claudio,' I shouted. 'Oh my God, please come on up with me to my place!' " (*SB* 31). Despite this equivocal invitation and unlike the unexpected encounters between males and lonely women in the fictional stories—the being from Saturn and the English spinster, the rich old lady and the pharmacy delivery boy—no erotic liaison ensues. This "man who appears" elicits from the narrator not eros, but a motherly concern. His feeble attempts at flirtation and romance are countered by her stern injunction that he must go home and get some sleep. Her empathy with him is greatest not because of their joint pursuit of literature (he is a talented poet, no longer able to write), but because of his failure: "Who, but *who* can say with sincerity that he has realized himself in this life? Success is a lie" (*SB* 33). Afterward, she continues to be haunted by the man's need:

> That was yesterday, Saturday. Today is Sunday, the twelfth of May. Mother's Day. How can I be a mother to this man? I ask myself and there is no answer.
> There is no answer to anything.
> I went to bed. I had died. (*SB* 35)

The burden that sympathetic mothering exacts is a sacrificial one, akin to the Christian sacrifice figured in the *via crucis* of the title. To save, or even only to want to save, requires a kind of death of the mothering subject. One of the impulses for narrative in Lispector is linked to this mothering function: although she cannot save the man, she can and does write about him. The sacrificial body of the title, *A via crucis do corpo*, is, in one sense, the body of the writer: to write is to imagine in one's flesh the sorrows of the world. "All the stories in this book are bruising stories," the narrator writes. "And I am the one who suffered most" (*SB* 3).

In the topsy-turvy world of the fictional stories and the "real life" they supposedly reflect, the role of the mother assumes a very different function. It no longer guarantees sexual propriety, and it may be filled by unlikely occupants who openly flaunt patriarchal law. At the end of "Explanation," the narrator says she refrained from writing yet another story for the book in order to protect the privacy of a simple man who had told her his life. His story, it turns out, features an illicit maternal sexuality, an adulterous wife who leads her daughter astray. Her son "doesn't even want to hear the sound of his own mother's name. And that's how things are" (*SB* 4). In "Plaza Mauá," the transvestite who earns his living from encounters with sailors at a nightclub is, in his private life, a true mother to his little adopted daughter. The nightclub "was full of men and women. Many mothers and housewives went there for the fun of it and to earn a bit of pocket money" (*SB* 57).

The most extended reference to motherhood occurs in "The Way of the Cross." This parody of the sacred story of the virgin birth shows the comic transfigurations of the unremarkable protagonists, who feel compelled to imitate the ancient narrative. The pregnant woman who insists that her husband had never touched her is convinced she will bear the Messiah. "Then I'm St. Joseph?" asks her startled husband. " 'You are,' was the laconic response" (*SB* 26).

Lispector's rewriting of the virgin birth goes against the ancient patriarchal mythic construct of "the virgin daughter as guardian of paternal power" (Kristeva 1986, 163). Julia Kristeva's analysis of the "virginal maternal" as, in one of its functions, a way of representing and holding in check female megalomania is pertinent here: "The Virgin assumes the paranoid lust for power by changing a woman into a Queen in heaven and a Mother of the earthly institution (of the Church). But she succeeds in stifling that megalomania by putting it on its knees before the child-god" (Kristeva 1986, 180). One of the traits of the myth of virgin birth is its inaccessibility to human mothers, who by definition are not virgins. Lispector's story matter-of-factly asserts both virginity and maternity. The woman is solely responsible for bringing forth her son, who will not rule over her, but will be subject, all too humanly, to the suffering shared by all: "No one knows if this child had to go the way of the cross. The way all go" (*SB* 29). In keeping with the challenges to patriarchy that underlie many of the sexual transgressions of the fictional stories, this rewriting of the sacred Christian story allows its female protagonist to indulge in megalomania. The intervention of the supernatural confers upon the woman the power to produce a child, triumphantly, without male participation.

The function of maternity differs widely, then, in the autobiographical and the fictional stories, yet it is the staid mother of the former who explicitly says she imagines the transgressive maternal sexuality of the latter. As we have seen in "The Egg and the Chicken" in chapter 3, any "mothering" that takes place in the realm of fiction is permeated by forces of violence and transgression. In *The Stations of the Body*, the impulses and desires of the autobiographical narrator are strikingly discontinuous with those revealed in the fictional stories. In "Explanation," the narrator insists on the mimetic power of literature, which demands of the writer a sacrificial attunement to the harshness of the world. As author, she does not bring into play her own desires, but instead guesses at reality. Although mocking serious fiction and the prestige of the institution of literature, Lispector attempts to maintain one aspect of the myth of the artist: the artist as privileged interpreter of reality, who sees more than common mortals can see. She falls back on this cultural myth to explain how she imagines the sordid incidents and characters the fictional stories display: "How do I know? I know. Artists know things" (*SB* 3). Yet Lispector ends the preface by calling into question this same supposed insight. In an abrupt and contradictory coda, the narrator suddenly denies her capacity to plumb other people's motives and secrets:

> I've tried to look closely into someone else's face—a cashier at the movies. In order to learn the secret of her life. Useless. The other person is an enigma. And with eyes that are those of a statue: blind. (*SB* 4)

This liminal figure, a guardian at the gates between life and narrative, disabuses the writer of her pretension to reveal the other. In her blind eyes—the blind eyes of a statue—the figure bears the wounds of the writer's own blindness. This grim disclaimer of the narrator's capacity to see the other stands as a warning to the reader who enters the world of these "stories that really happened" and that claim to reveal secret, embarrassing, fantastic, or even criminal moments of other people's sexual lives.

Whose impulse, then, whose desire does the writer follow when she writes? What is the relation of the fictional imagination to the unseemliness of social life? Does the writer tell the "truth" about other beings? Or is this truth hopelessly compromised and limited by the pressure of the writer's own desires? If the writer is unable to reveal reality, she is left with two disquieting options: she either reveals herself and her own fantasies, or else she simply sets in circulation once again already established and financially successful fictional formulas. Over either possibility looms the shadow of a base commercialism, an immoral sale. The opposite of the writer as mother, the reverse of the maternal metaphor, would be the writer as prostitute. Prostitution appears frequently in the fictional stories of this collection and is hinted at as a threatening, rejected metaphor for the exchange between writer and reader: "I just want to make clear that I don't write for money but rather on impulse. . . . I'm an honorable woman" (*SB* 3). Sylvia Plath, another writer of high art who, as Jacqueline Rose shows in a recent book, was irresistibly drawn to writing popular fiction—in her case, sentimental stories for women published in women's magazines—also confronts the image of the prostitute when she considers the writing of popular fiction. Plath writes in her journal: "My supercilious attitude about people who write confessions has diminished. It takes a good tight plot and a slick ease that are not picked up overnight like a cheap whore" (Rose 1991, 170). Writing confessions takes professional skills, Plath argues, and is not equivalent to consorting with, much less *being*, a cheap whore.

For Lispector, the specter of an immoral sale is not easily set aside. If a writer writes for money, what does she sell? This question disturbed Lispector, as she reveals in one of her first few *crônicas* for the *Jornal do Brasil* (September 9, 1967):

> Besides being a beginner in the matter of writing "crônicas," I'm also a beginner in writing to earn money. I've worked in journalism as a

professional without a byline. But when I sign my name I become automatically more personal. And I feel a little as if I were selling my soul. I mentioned this to a friend, who said: but writing is always a little like selling one's soul. It's true. Even when you are not doing it for money, you reveal a great deal about yourself. . . . I sell, therefore, to you, with the greatest pleasure, a certain part of my soul—the part for Saturday conversations. (Lispector 1992, 42)

Whereas the *crônista* easily comes to terms with selling a public part of her soul, the writer of sensational narratives may implicate the integrity of her art or the privacy of her desires by marketing sexual fantasies. Like the prostitute, she sells as a commodity a supposedly priceless or intimate part of herself. The view of writing as mimetic and of the writer as the sacrificial mother who suffers as she reveals reality serves in a sense as a protection against the more disquieting implications of writing on sexual themes. Yet, in the autobiographical narratives, the narrator also chafes at the constrictions of "proper" writing and hints at the reckless desire to try her hand at a fiction that would bypass subtleties, reach a wider audience, and perhaps bring in more money.

Lispector's autobiographical narrator fears and desires a different mode of fiction, just as her repressed characters fear and desire sexual experience. And just as Miss Algrave and other characters embrace with a sort of vengeful joy the lifting of repressions, so too does the narrator embrace her transgressive fictions. In "Explanation," the editor who provokes Lispector to follow her own hidden inspiration is cast in a position similar to that of various males in subsequent stories—the being from outer space and the two rapists on the train—whose words or actions reveal to women their own unacknowledged desires. "I told him I didn't know how to write commissioned stories. But—even as he talked to me on the phone—I began to feel inspiration growing in me" (*SB* 3).

The play of echoes and shadows between the autobiographical and the fictional stories reveals a woman writer struggling with her female gender role as it intersects with the public and private dimensions of her writing: its performance in the literary marketplace, its possible monetary value, its pliability to the demands of an editor, its continuation of or inferiority to earlier literary achievements, its responsiveness or blindness to the "real life" it purports to reveal, its enmeshment with the author's own desires. In addition to experimenting with radically different styles of language and plot, Lispector takes further than ever before the construction of the character as other, apparently far removed from her social, economic, and psychic world.

In much of Lispector's earlier fiction, her questing characters are all, it has been argued, versions and reflections of one another and an exacerbated manifestation of Flaubert's dictum: "Madame Bovary, c'est moi."[11] The truth of Lispector's characters, Benedito Nunes affirms, naming several of her protagonists, "is the truth of the writer, possessor of the passion for existence and language that she delegates to them" (Nunes 1973, 151). The protagonist-narrator of *The Stream of Life* is perhaps an extreme example of Lispector's strategy for setting up characters as authorial surrogates, a term I borrow from Neil Hertz. In an essay on George Eliot, he identifies "instances of a distribution of attributes operating within the fictional world of the novel: images that . . . George Eliot in letters [applies] to her own inner life are attached, as in a medieval psychomachia, to separate characters in the narratives" (Hertz 1985, 81-82). In Lispector's case, her autobiographical narratives, her pieces on writing, and her fiction present protagonists engaged in inquiries so remarkably similar that she often, as we have seen, lifts pieces from the nonfictional texts and inserts them in her fictions.

The characters in the fictional stories of *The Stations of the Body* might at first seem to be located at the opposite end of the continuum, far removed from the vertiginous doublings and mirrorings that take place between author, narrator, and characters in works such as *The Stream of Life*. In *The Stations of the Body*, Lispector indeed draws freely from literary modes that set characters at a distance and even mock them, such as comedy and farce. These fictional stories, however, are mingled with the autobiographical ones, thus raising a number of intriguing issues. Whereas the fictional stories and some of the explicit metafictional reflections place the characters firmly in the realm of the "not me," the more subtle implications of the narratives of the collection, taken as a whole, call into question that distinction and allow us to read the book as a continuation—although in a comic and parodic register—of the central concerns of Lispector's fiction. Here, too, self and other prove to be not entirely distinct, but, rather, open to mutual encroachments, as Lispector with irony and unsparing wit follows the migrations of desire between the two permeable realms of autobiography and fiction.

5
Rape and Textual Violence

Persistently, from her earliest fiction, Lispector imagines stories about characters construed as victims.[1] In *Near to the Wild Heart*, in *Family Ties*, and elsewhere, she turns an acute gaze to the exercise of personal power, to the push and pull of the strong and the weak, and particularly to the dynamics of victimization. Usually, but not always, the victims are female; sometimes the line between victim and victimizer blurs, or, in a sudden reversal, the two exchange places. In Lispector's early short story collections, such as *Family Ties* (1960), the family is the site of many of these battles. Victims are created by the vagaries of personal affections, the will-to-power that love hides and sanctions, and the rigidities of male/female relations as constructed by a particular society. At other times, Lispector places these interpersonal struggles in the broader context of the individual subject's contact with impersonal cosmic forces, termed "reality" or "God" (although not in any conventional religious sense); this contact does not seem to be entirely voluntary, it is often fraught with violence, and it may be cast as an interaction between self and other. In one of Lispector's best-known novels, *The Passion according to G.H.* (1964), this "reality" inheres in a cockroach: a female narrator watches it closely, kills it, and then, in a sort of mystical communion, tastes its substance. In this tense encounter, observation yields repulsion, identification, and dizzying reversals of relative power as the woman feels engulfed by the cockroach, which is in turn victimizer and victim. I think it fair to say that in Lispector narrative often demands a victim, or, conversely, that the victim demands narrative.[2]

But how, from what perspective, and with what investments does one write the victim's experience? Lispector gives two divergent answers to this question in her writing. The first can be seen in three short narratives that clearly define the victims: young women who are raped or attacked in various ways. In these stories, Lispector distances and naturalizes violence against women, presenting their victimization as an inevitable part of the way things are. A second and more radical consideration of the dynamics of victimization can be seen in the last narrative Lispector published before her death, *The Hour of the Star* (1977): here, the strategy for writing the victim no longer entails a containment within ideological and narrative structures that minimize the violence, but involves, on the contrary, an unleashing of aggressive forces. Whereas the earlier rape stories show the workings of representation as a construct that further oppresses the victims by diminishing and justifying the assaults they suffer, *The Hour of the Star* foregrounds and calls into question the perverse components of the pleasures of writing and reading and the suspect alliances of narrative with forces of mastery and domination.

I

The three stories about sexual assault, "Mystery in São Cristóvão," "Preciousness," and "Pig Latin," the only representations of rape among the many instances of transgressive sexuality and physical violence in her fiction, depict a symbolic, a partial, and a deflected rape. She wrote these stories at different stages in her career, and collected them in volumes published in 1952, 1960, and 1974, respectively.

In the earliest story, "Mystery in São Cristóvão," published in *Family Ties* (1960; *Alguns contos*, 1952), a third-person narrator tells of the encounter in a lyrical and tranquilizing tone. The violence, mostly psychological (its slight symbolic manifestation deflected onto an object), occurs in the setting of a family's home in a middle-class neighborhood of Rio. Late at night, three young men on their way to a party, dressed up as a rooster, a bull, and a knight with a devil's mask, trespass into "the forbidden territory of the garden" (*FT* 135) to steal some hyacinths. They have barely broken the stalk of one flower when the "defloration" begins. "Behind the dark glass of the window, a white face was watching them" (*FT* 137). The men feel as frightened as the young woman who watches them. "None of the four knew who was punishing whom. The hyacinths seemed to become whiter in the darkness. Paralyzed, they stood staring at each other" (*FT* 137). The encounter provokes deep but unspecified resonances in each participant. The young woman, whose white face becomes *her* mask, appears no more a victim than the trespassers. "The simple encounter of four masks in that autumn evening seemed to have touched deep recesses, then others, then still others" (*FT* 136). This ritualistic confrontation, although not naming the specific motive for the powerful feelings, hints that they spring from the fascination with and fear of sexual contact.

Although fear strikes all four, the confrontation touches the young woman most deeply. She leaves the window and screams, but can explain nothing to her alarmed family:

> Her face grew small and bright—the whole laborious structure of her years had dissolved and she was a child once more. But in her rejuvenated image, to the horror of her family, a white strand had appeared among the hairs of her forehead. (*FT* 137)

The white hyacinth, her white face, and, finally, the white strand of hair represent the vulnerable female body that bears the marks of the assault. It is the grandmother, "her white hair in braids," who finds the only "visible sign" of the incident: "the hyacinth—still alive but with its stalk broken" (*FT* 137-38). The young men, also shaken, cling together at the party, "their speechless faces beneath three masks which faltered independently" (*FT* 137). Their costumes seem a flimsy facade of masculinity. The hyacinths—"tall, hard and fragile" (*FT* 135)—also have a phallic import: the initiation involves a fearful rupture and is curiously disempowering for both sexes. The four characters act in the grip of an impersonal force, which surges from their "hollow recesses," yet seems somehow alien, like their masks. In a convergence of culture and nature, masks and inner forces work together to determine the actions of the uncomprehending and frightened subjects. The characters come to no rational understanding of the encounter; the violation remains unacknowledged, unspoken. The young woman soon forgets or represses whatever the confrontation led her to intuit (the better to proceed with the "real" violations it foreshadows?): "She gradually recovered her true years" (*FT* 138).

In this encounter, a mysterious violence aligns itself with inner and outer nature, appearing as natural as the evening, the moon, and the flowers. The masks of masculine aggressiveness represent cultural roles, but their animal guises (rooster, bull) link them back to nature, and the mythic figure (devil) stands for equally unquestioned psychic impulses. Distance and impersonality characterize the narrative mode of this story. The narrator stands back from the nameless characters to tell of their actions. In the postsymbolist climate of this theatrical, stylized, and aesthetically pleasing world, masks, sounds, looks, and the play of light and darkness bear suggestive meanings. The encroachment upon a woman's body, with its repercussion for the aggressors, seems justified as an inevitable part of growing up, and as a component of the postsymbolist repertoire that the narrative deploys.

"Preciousness" (*Family Ties*, 1960), a longer and more complex story, takes up again an initiatory encounter between strangers. Two frightened but predatory young men briefly attack an adolescent on her way to school in the darkness of early morning by reaching out to touch her body. A third-person narrative, unwaveringly centered on the young woman, conveys her feelings and fantasies, and "reads" those of the young men only in the sound of their footsteps and in their gestures. The sexual assault is embedded in a subtle and many-layered account of the girl's adolescent conflicts. Timidity and arrogance, pride and shame in her body, sexual curiosity and revulsion, gender role rebellion and compliance alternately determine her thoughts and actions. The narrative follows a double movement. First, it presents the girl's daily routine of going to school and back, when the fear of a sexual attack weaves through her thoughts. Second, the narrative retraces that routine on one specific day, when an attack in fact does take place. As in the first story, the violation, rather slight in its outer manifestation, occurs in a dreamy atmosphere. It is as if inner fantasies and outer events converged: the girl on her way to school spends an hour of "daydreams as acute as a crime" (*FT* 103).

Questions of power, gender, and sexuality are at the center of this story. The "preciousness" of the title refers to the girl's feelings about herself, which echo and prolong society's positive valuing of nubile virgins. Yet she is precious to herself mainly for other reasons:

> She was fifteen years old and she was not pretty. But inside her thin body
> existed an almost majestic vastness in which she stirred, as in a
> meditation. And within the mist there was something precious. Which did
> not extend itself, did not compromise itself nor contaminate itself. Which
> was intense like a jewel. Herself. (*FT* 102)

If she is precious or interesting to men as a brand-new sexual object, untouched and touchable, she is precious to herself for an as yet imprecise but "vast" potential that she protects by her aloof, self-enclosed manner. The girl's newly developed body bestows upon her an untapped "vast" power over men, yet also results in a new sort of vulnerability to sexual advances.

Although the girl mainly fears the milder and more common assaults by looks or words (She considers even men's thoughts invasive and wishes to control them), in this incident she suffers an attack by touch. As the two men approach her, she feels compelled not to turn and flee from an encounter where pride and power are at issue. The narrator describes the girl with a kind of respectful exaltation: she walks on "heroic legs," "with a firm gait, her mouth set, moving in her Spanish rhythm" (*FT* 108). Her courage is more than courage: "It was the gift. And the great vocation for a destiny. She advanced, suffering as she obeyed" (*FT* 108). It is as if this assault followed a predetermined plan, to which the individuals involved must submit. Yet the attackers overstep the boundaries of that plan:

What followed were four awkward hands, four hands that did not know what they wanted, four mistaken hands of people with no vocation, four hands that touched her so unexpectedly that she did the best thing that she could have done in the world of movement: she became paralyzed. They, whose premeditated part was merely that of passing alongside the darkness of her fear, and then the first of the seven mysteries would collapse; they . . . had failed to understand their function and, with the individuality of those who experience fear, they had attacked. It had lasted less than a fraction of a second in that quiet street. Within a fraction of a second, they touched her as if all seven mysteries belonged to them. Which she preserved in their entirety and became the more a larva and fell seven more years behind. (*FT* 110)

In this ritual gone wrong, the error seems to lie in the rush to appropriate too many mysteries too soon. Only youth, awkwardness, lack of understanding and vocation characterize these anonymous attackers, presented with remarkable sympathy and some disdain. "From the haste with which they wounded her, she realized that they were more frightened than she was" (*FT* 110). Where and how they "wound" her remains unspecified, but the impact seems severe. The attack at first impedes the girl's inner growth; she "falls behind" and experiences a paralysis on which the narrative dwells at length.

The assault seems to have proved to her that she is not, after all, precious to anyone else. Alone in the school lavatory, she cries out loud: "I am alone in the world! No one will ever help me, no one will ever love me! I am all alone in the world!" (*FT* 112). She has exchanged the solitude of the special being, the elect, for the solitude of someone whose power has been cut back. She moves out of the world of missions and sacrifices; the narrative abandons those aggrandizing metaphors. As she looks in the mirror to comb her hair, she sees herself as an enclosed animal: "The expression of her nose was that of a snout, peeping through a fence" (*FT* 113). The certainty of the disparity between her external and internal value moves her to practical gestures of self-protection, which includes demanding of her family new shoes: "Mine make a lot of noise, a woman can't walk on wooden heels, it attracts too much attention!" (*FT* 113). This request reconnects her obliquely to the assault. As the men approached her, she focused her fear on the sound of their footsteps and of her own. By demanding new shoes, she counters the insight that followed the violation: she extracts tangible proof of her family's love and care. The "quiet" shoes would put her in a relationship of dissimilarity, both to her own previous self and to her assailants. By associating "quiet" with womanliness she internalizes a traditional feature of femininity and seems to give up her fantasies of specialness and power (Lindstrom 1982, 193). Yet the language of ritual returns in the paragraph that concludes the story with an almost celebratory tone:

Until, just as a person grows fat, she ceased, without knowing by what process, to be precious. There is an obscure law which decrees that the egg be protected until the chick is born, a bird of fire. And she got her new shoes. (*FT* 113)

The attack seems to begin a process that ultimately results in the loss of her preciousness, now appearing as a self-protective fantasy, and in the girl's recognition of her true vulnerability as a woman and human being. Sexual assault, here as in the first story, is mitigated by appeals to "obscure laws" that govern human nature and social conduct. The attack nudges forward the protagonist's growth: the suffering of violence brings with it inner progress and social adaptation, turning ugly chick into "bird of fire."

The story "Pig Latin," published in *The Stations of the Body* (*A via crucis do corpo*, 1974), is an example of Lispector's later short narratives, where the plot enacts literally the violence previously contained in her characters' feelings and fantasies and in the figurative language that describes them. The stories are brief, brisk, their simple syntax and occasional vulgarisms a stark contrast to the involutions and periphrases of Lispector's earlier style. They also dismiss the psychological scrutiny at the center of her earlier work. Yet this story about rape repeats in a different register certain configurations of the two earlier ones. It is also a violent initiation because the protagonist, Cidinha, is on the brink of entering a larger world. An English teacher from the provinces, she is traveling to the metropolis: first Rio, then New York. Two men sitting opposite her in the train look her over and begin talking to each other in a strange language. Suddenly she understands that they are speaking pig latin, planning to rape her in the tunnel and kill her if she tries to resist. She does not consider using this advance warning—pig latin was the language "they had used as children to protect themselves from the grownups" (*SB* 60)—to defend herself; getting up and changing places might have been enough. Her response is more devious:

If I pretend that I am a prostitute they'll give up, they wouldn't want a whore.
So she pulled up her skirt, made sensual movements she didn't even know she knew how to make, so unknown was she to herself—and opened the top buttons on her blouse, leaving her breasts half exposed. The men suddenly in shock.
"Eshay's razycay."
In other words, "she's crazy." (*SB* 61)

This act of self-defense masked as seduction reveals the hidden motives of the men. Cidinha correctly sees that they desire not sexual pleasure but inflicting cruelty and humiliation. When she offers to give freely (or perhaps for a fee) what they were about to take, the men are amused and put off. The ticket collector also takes her for a prostitute and she is turned over to the police. Because, like other of Lispector's protagonists, she cannot explain—"How could she explain pig latin?" (*SB* 62)—she spends three days in jail:

> Finally they let her go. She took the next train to Rio. She had washed her face. She wasn't a prostitute any more. What bothered her was this: when the two had spoken of raping her, she had wanted to be raped. She was shameless. Danay Iay maay aay orewhay. That was what she had discovered. Humiliation. (*SB* 62)

When she left the train under arrest, still in her prostitute guise, a young woman about to board looked at her with scorn. Several days later, Cidinha comes upon a newspaper headline: "Girl Raped and Killed in Train." The presumably virtuous and unyielding young woman dies at the same assailants' hands. Cidinha saves herself by pretending to be what, in her own severe self-judgment, she really is.

Her successful strategy hinges on the recognition of her double oppression in society. She is "rapable" to the extent that she is "pure," for in order to be a particularly desirable object of sexual violence, she must have done prior violence to herself, by suppressing her own sexuality. Yet Cidinha agrees with her attackers, complicitly acquiescing in the brutal equations that oppress women: having sexual desires equals being a whore; wanting sexual contact equals wanting to be raped. The men still manage to humiliate her by making her aware of her sexual desires.

The protagonist's escape is a small battle won in a losing war. After she reads the headlines, "she trembled all over":

> It had happened, then. And to the girl who had despised her.
>   She began to cry there in the street. She threw away the damned newspaper. She didn't want to know the details.
>   "Atefay siay placableimay."
>   Fate is implacable. (*SB* 62)

The protagonist's complicity with a gender ideology that oppresses her becomes clear in her adoption of the rapists' pig latin. In it, she accuses herself of being a whore, and sees the rape and murder of her substitute not as the result of certain human arrangements but as an instance of implacable fate. The naturalization of violence persists in this story. No longer seen as a ritual that helps girls and boys grow up, the confrontation with sexual violence has now become an initiation into the brutality a woman faces in the "real world" by virtue of her gender. The men's own fear, their youth, or their compliance with mysterious "obscure laws" no longer mitigate the violence displayed by the assailants, who are briefly and stereotypically described: "One was tall, thin, with a little mustache and a cold eye, the other was short, paunchy, and bald" (*SB* 68). Although these two are certainly the most ridiculous, and are made fools of by the girl (who does not thereby permanently disarm them), all the men come off badly in these stories, even the earlier, more sympathetically described assailants. The configuration of two or three men against one woman at first seems an obvious symbol of the unequal balance of power between the sexes. In the unfolding of the stories, however, the numerical imbalance also points to the weakness of men, who gather together for strength in order to impose their dominance. The protagonist of "Pig Latin" manages only to deflect the violence. The farcical elements here, especially the comic improbability of a plot that has criminals speaking pig latin, serve as a distancing device in a story that proceeds as a morality tale, laying bare the cruel workings of a rigidly unjust world.

II

These three narratives figure sexual assault in a progression that goes from a mildly toned and "aesthetic" symbolic representation to literal and farcical plot events. Yet all the stories share narrative devices that minimize violence. Effaced third-person narrators interpret the victim's experience, while never implicating themselves in the violent acts. There are no encoded readers; these texts suggest for their reception the position of discreet, impersonal observation. These stories focus on specific incidents of aggression, which are explained and assimilated by ideologies about personal growth, adolescent sexual fantasies, initiation into the harshness of male-female relations, and woman's place in a world governed by "implacable fate." *The Hour of the Star*, the ninety-page novella Lispector published just months before her death, offers a new and challenging perspective on writing the victim, where violence is no longer naturalized and contained. In this work, Lispector represents overlapping systems of oppression and a victim absolutely crushed by them. At the same time, she accuses writer, narrator, and reader of participating in and profiting from that oppression.

In an elaborate fiction within a fiction, the narrator of *The Hour of the Star*, a male writer, discusses his creation of a female protagonist. This young woman, a bona fide social victim, is a native of the Northeast, a region that, in its tortured landscape and harsh reality of droughts and severe economic ills, has attracted the imagination of many Brazilian writers. The protagonist, recently arrived in Rio, hungry, marginalized, displaced, represents others in her situation, a fragment of a vast social reality. In this text, Lispector opens up the scope of her depiction of the experience of oppression beyond the scrutiny of gender-role conflicts and spiritual crises of middle-class women (and the occasional man). Simultaneously, she calls into question the process whereby literature represents oppression.

The protagonist, Macabéa, a barely literate typist who has joined the urban poor of Rio, belongs to an underworld of those living in cramped quarters and subservience in exchange for enough to eat. Her improbable job as a typist—this text also has many farcical elements—provides her with a modicum of dignity, but exposes her to ridicule because she types word for word and cannot spell. An orphan, her growth stunted by poverty, Macabéa was raised by an aunt who enjoyed beating her. Chaste, proud of her virginity, she murmurs each morning: "I'm a typist and a virgin, and I like Coca-Cola" (*HS* 35).[3] She confides to her boyfriend an incongruous dream: "Do you know what I really want to be? A movie star. . . . Did you know that Marilyn Monroe was the color of peaches?— "And you're the color of mud," her boyfriend retorts. "You haven't got the face or the body to be a movie star" (*HS* 53). Macabéa, moreover, is infertile: "Her ovaries are as shrivelled as overcooked mushrooms" (*HS* 58). Yet she is sensuous without knowing it. 'How could so much sensuality," the narrator asks, "fit in a body as withered as hers without her even suspecting its presence?" (*HS* 73). With the rude bluntness of caricature, Lispector makes clear that Macabéa is victimized by everything and everyone: her brutal aunt broke her spirit, poverty weakens her body, her boyfriend insults her; at the same time patriarchy neutralizes her sensuality, and foreign stereotypes of beauty encourage her and others to despise her appearance. The movies also provide an outlet for her self-hate: "Macabéa had a passion for musicals and horror films. She especially liked films where women were hanged or shot through the heart with a bullet" (*HS* 58). Macabéa is "raped," not by one individual man, but by a multitude of social and cultural forces that conspire to use her cruelly for the benefit of others.

The plot takes Macabéa through a series of large and small misfortunes, which relentlessly beat her down. First, her boss puts her on notice that she is to be fired. Next begins a desultory courtship, in which Macabéa is the object of Olímpico's insults and an audience for his fantasies of grandeur. He soon abandons her to take up with her office mate Glória. Finally, a fortune-teller predicts for Macabéa a happy ending, complete with marriage to a rich gringo. But this Cinderella outcome is no sooner suggested than it is brutally cut short. Stepping out of the fortune-teller's house, Macabéa meets her death in a hit-and-run accident: the gringo, driving a Mercedes, turns out to be her killer, not her groom.[4]

On one level, then, these "feeble adventures of a young woman in a city all set up against her" (*HS* 15) compose a plot that parodies the sentimental stories of ill-used innocence and shattered dreams in many literary and nonliterary texts. On another level, this novella, "a fiction of fiction making" in Peter Brooks's term (1986, 315), concerns itself with narration, especially with the possibility of mimesis and with the charged authorial investments in the creation of characters. We are given not only the story of the victim, but also a meditation on writing the victim, a process that itself duplicates and inscribes the act of victimization.

Macabéa is both a grotesque other and a repository for subtle processes of identification by which the narrator claims to gain access to her interiority and her reality. "I use myself as a form of knowledge," the narrator remarks, addressing Macabéa. "I know you to the bone by means of an incantation that comes from me to you" (*HS* 82). Macabéa herself does not engage in quests. She lacks practical ambitions and insight into what the narrator claims is her "true" condition. Her inwardness is empty: "She was only vaguely aware of a kind of absence of herself in herself. If she were someone who could communicate her feelings, she would say: the world is beyond me, I am beyond myself" (*HS* 24). The narrator is the questing character, who pursues a verbal construct: writing the victim's story and through it, his own. "Even though I have nothing to do with this young woman, I will have to write myself through her, amazed at every turn" (*HS* 24).

In the dramatization of the storytelling act, three textual interactions emerge as central. All are unstable and often aggressive, hinging on identification and rejection, sympathy and repulsion: first, the implicit connection between Lispector and her male narrator, Rodrigo S. M. (given the context of cruelty, it is difficult not to think of the sadomasochism these initials sometimes signify); second, the narrator's relationship with Macabéa, whom he invents, but whose "truth" he also claims to "capture"; third, the interaction between Rodrigo S. M. and the encoded reader, whom he frequently—and contentiously—addresses. References to narration fragment the plot, interrupting it on almost every page. There is nothing seamless about the text, and much that is abrupt, excessive, and grotesque. The grid through which Macabéa is written, itself fictional, of course, remains firmly in the foreground.

The autobiographical references that from the mid-1960s on frequently intrude in Lispector's fictional narratives, disrupting systematically the fictional pretense with what we might call the autobiographical pretense, here appear in the preface, "Dedication by the Author (actually, Clarice Lispector)." Lispector assumes a masculine voice and makes the preface stylistically indistinguishable from Rodrigo S. M.'s narrative. If her narrator is a mask, Lispector seems to imply, then so is her autobiographical "self." The preface begins:

> Thus, I dedicate this thing here to Schumann of long ago and his sweet Clara, who are now bones, woe to us. I dedicate myself to a shade of red, very scarlet like my blood of a man in his prime and therefore I dedicate myself to my blood. (*HS* 7)

In these dizzying reversals of subject/object relations, the disdain implicit in "I dedicate this thing here" quickly subsides and the verb becomes reflexive: "I dedicate myself." The giving of something external to someone else collapses, in a vertigo of self-involvement, into the giving of oneself to oneself (but also to a male other residing in one's very blood). These alternations of rejection and identification between the first person, the text, and those whom it addresses continue to be dramatized as points of friction in the novella. But why, we might ask, the equivocal cross-gender connections between Lispector and her male narrator? She gives him a masculine identity, he gives *her* male blood: "my blood of a man in his prime." The author is a woman who assumes a male mask and the narrator, the mask of a female author. The blurring of gender demarcations continues in the novella when the narrator in turn creates a fictional female as his mask and his double. The insistent recourse to a male subject of discourse—both in the autobiographical preface and in the fictional narrative—functions as a distancing device that opens up textual space for various kinds of irony. Rodrigo S. M. again and again refuses the rhetoric of pity and facilitates the narrator's broad repertory of emotions, including negative ones, toward Macabéa. To this end, his individuality may be irrelevant, but his gender matters:

> Come to think of it, I discover now that I am not at all necessary either and what I write another could write. Another writer, yes, but it would have to be a man because a woman writer might get all tearful and cloying. (*HS* 14)

With irony, Lispector at once curiously rejects and endorses the cultural myth of the sentimental woman writer. Although the "real" author is of course a female writer, she insists that the fictive author must be male. The male mask, by increasing the distance between narrator and character, also points up the outrageous presumption that writing the other, especially the oppressed other, implies. "It is my passion to be the other. In this instance, the female other. I tremble, emaciated, filthy, just like her" (*HS* 29).

The interaction between Rodrigo S. M. and Macabéa, the most pressing concern of the metatextual commentary, entails two main issues. The first is a sustained, although partly implicit, questioning of the status of a novelist's invention of fictional characters. How much of it originates in valid apprehension of personal and social truth, as the narrator in his more optimistic moments believes? "Can it be that it's my painful task to imagine in my own flesh the truth that no one wants to face?" (*HS* 56). Writing, in this view a generous gift, gives voice to those who would otherwise be silent. In much of the metatextual commentary, mimesis appears urgent and attainable.

A second set of metatextual commentaries contradicts the possibility of mimesis, or at least sees representation as more complicated and charged. One obstacle to mimesis stems from class differences between narrator and characters. These disparities in economic status and cultural presuppositions are not smoothed over, but are played up as points of friction. Prejudice, repugnance, fear, and guilt animate the cruelty so pervasive in this text, lodging, for instance in the narrator's remarks about the street where Macabéa lives: "Acre Street. What a place. The big fat rats of Acre Street. I wouldn't go there for the world because I'm shamelessly terrified of that drab piece of filthy life" (*HS* 30). The narrator constructs Macabéa and the other characters by calling upon openly displayed class prejudices. The characterization of Olímpico and Glória, especially, relies with strident glee on the clichés through which the upper classes typically view the poor: Olímpico's gold tooth, proudly acquired, and greasy hair ointment; Glória's cheap perfume disguising infrequent baths, her bleached egg-yellow hair.

Other pressures also undercut social mimesis and intrude into the narrator's resolve to see Macabéa. How much of the novelist's invention originates in the murkier waters of self-concern? In self-seeking, self-abasing, expiatory, or malevolent investments? The narrator loses focus on his protagonist, and deviously, compulsively, he replaces her: "I see [Macabéa] looking in the mirror and—the ruffle of a drum—in the mirror my face appears, weary and unshaven. So thoroughly do we take each other's place" (*HS* 22).

Images of victim and victimizer alternately define the relationship between narrator and Macabéa. His masculine gender allows for double entendres that sometimes propose for this "liaison" the model of a typically exploitative sexual affair between a man and a woman of disparate social circumstances: "Before this typist entered my life, I was a reasonably cheerful man" (*HS* 17). Although the social context of his discourse may implicate him as the exploiter, he often sees himself as victim. "Well, the typist doesn't want to get off my back. Why me, of all people? I find out that as I had suspected poverty is ugly and promiscuous" (*HS* 21). Although Macabéa in the text's fiction knows nothing of her narrator—like Borges's dreamer in "The Circular Ruins" she believes she is real—she possesses a peculiar power as a site for the narrator's investments. Provoking his guilt, forcing him to live in her skin, she drags him through the misfortunes he invents for her. The attraction of the narrator to Macabéa is compulsive, involuntary. Lispector offers this equivocal commerce between narrator and character as a parable on a basic motivation of narrative and on the obstacles to social mimesis.

Two contradictory but interwoven languages govern Macabéa's characterization. The language of the grotesque fixes Macabéa's life and appearance in cruelly degrading poses, but is periodically displaced by another language that rewrites her in lyrical terms. Narrator and characters seem equally drawn to defining Macabéa in disparaging metaphorical and descriptive epithets, which favor essentializing predicates following the verb "to be." The following quotations are representative of the narrator's deflating definitions:

She was all rather dingy, for she rarely washed. (*HS* 26)

Nobody looked at her in the street; she was like a cup of cold coffee. (*HS* 27)

She was born with a bad record and looked like a child of who knows what, with an air of apologizing for taking up space. (*HS* 26)

> She was a chance event. A fetus thrown in the garbage, wrapped in newspaper. (*HS* 36)
>
> She had no fat and her whole organism was dry like a half empty sack of crumbled toast. (*HS* 38)

Other chararacters contribute to this insistent chorus. "You, Macabéa, are like a hair in a bowl of soup," her former boyfriend tells her. "No one feels like eating it" (*HS* 60). This generalized textual impulse to demean the protagonist continues down to the scene of her death:

> Did she suffer? I believe so. Like a chicken with a clumsily severed neck, running around in a panic, dripping blood. Except that the chicken flees, as one flees from pain, with horrified cluckings. And Macabéa struggled in silence. (*HS* 80)

Bakhtin, in a chapter of his book on Rabelais, points out that "of all the features of the human face, the nose and mouth play the most important part in the grotesque image of the body" (Bakhtin 1968, 316). Although she usually employs images of absence, insubstantiality, and lack to define Macabéa, Lispector, in two mirror scenes, contrives to provide her with a grotesque nose and mouth. In the bathroom of her office building, it seems to Macabéa at first that the dull and darkened mirror reflects nothing at all:

> Could it be that her physical existence had disappeared? This illusion soon passed and she saw her whole face distorted by the cheap mirror, her enormous nose like the cardboard nose of a clown. (*HS* 24-25)

A later mirror scene, which similarly stresses this text's attachment to a deforming mimesis, focuses on her mouth. She puts on bright-red lipstick, purposely going beyond the contours of her thin lips, in a futile attempt to resemble Marilyn Monroe. Afterward,

> she stood staring in the mirror at the face staring back in astonishment. It seemed that instead of lipstick thick blood oozed from her lips, as if someone had punched her in the mouth, broken her teeth and torn her flesh. (*HS* 61-62)

Blood and vomit, obsessively frequent in this text, signal the opening up of the body and the rupture of its self-enclosed system. Like other "acts performed on the confines of the body and the outer world," bleeding and vomiting contribute to the grotesque image of the body as Bakhtin describes it (1968, 317). Macabéa suffers from permanent hunger and equally permanent nausea, indexes of her position in a world she cannot incorporate and that refuses to accept her. Blood and vomit mark the hour of her death, which the narrator had mistakenly predicted would bring her a moment of glory:

> She would surely die one day as if beforehand she had learned by heart
> how to play the star. For at the hour of death a person becomes a brilliant
> movie star, it's every one's moment of glory. (*HS* 28)

The promise of stardom—of height, of exaltation—is reversed, debased, materializing in a star-shaped pool of blood on the pavement. Eating (and the contrasting states of hunger and nausea), several forms of elimination, and bleeding, dispersed throughout the text, point up Macabéa's pathetic lack of glory and adaptation in contrast to the other characters' vigorous, if repugnant, incorporation into and of the world.

In counterpoint to this grotesque inscription of Macabéa, an equally insistent, though less dominant, language of lyricism emerges. The narrator exalts her, proclaims his affection:

> Yes, I'm in love with Macabéa, my darling Maca, in love with her
> homeliness and total anonymity, for she belongs to no one at all. In love
> with her fragile lungs, the scrawny little thing. (*HS* 68)

Her physical thinness at times becomes airy, delicate. He reveals her spiritual bent: she has faith, believes in the goodness of others, and falls into ecstatic states upon contemplating a rainbow or a particular play of light, hearing Caruso sing on the radio, or looking at a tree. Her subjectivity is not entirely empty, after all. Yet it is through her inner emptiness that she approaches saintliness: "Most of the time she possessed without knowing it the emptiness that fills the soul of saints. Was she a saint? It would seem so" (*HS* 37). Irony lurks at the edges of this lyrical language, but does not totally undercut its effect. In sketching Macabéa, the text proceeds by disconcerting juxtapositions of the "high" and the "low," in the plot, in descriptions, and in clusters of metaphors. These contradictory forces of exaltation and abasement, which at times include a gratuitous violence, appear again and again.

Berta Waldman, one of Lispector's insightful readers, remarks about Macabéa:

> In her simple nature, she represents a being without fissures, continuous
> with herself, who exists at the center of the savage heart [an allusion to
> Lispector's first novel, *Near to the Wild Heart*] in the paradisiacal space
> where beings participate in the inner nucleus of things, a space which
> proved impenetrable to Lispector's other characters. (Waldman 1983, 69)

Waldman accounts here for only one side of Macabéa's portrayal, an unstable one at that, for Macabéa's paradisiacal self-identity is not constant. The critic neglects to acknowledge how irony and the grotesque constantly undercut her presentation as a being without fissures. In one sense, however, and this is an aspect of the text some readers may find offensive, Macabéa is a privileged soul when set against the gallery of Lispector's seekers of truth and inner harmony. Her simplemindedness attenuates anguish and self-division; she believes she is happy. As the quintessentially vulnerable being, ideally open to existence, she possesses, like a holy fool, an unsought, unconscious wisdom. Macabéa's musings echo those of Lispector's serious thinkers, with a parodic edge, in terms significantly askew. Curious about the cultural artifacts that surround and yet escape her, she collects odd bits of information and words whose meanings she does not know ("algebra," "electronic," "culture," "ephemeris"). She asks questions, both weighty and idiotic, without necessarily expecting answers:

> How do I manage to make myself possible? (*HS* 48)
>
> Is the sky above or below? (*HS* 31)

In his own tortured way, the narrator also questions and despairs of finding answers:

> As long as I have questions to which there are no answers, I'll go on writing. (*HS* 11)
>
> This book is a silence. This book is a question. (*HS* 17)

And Lispector, in turn, also refracts this same questioning mode when she writes in the preface:

> This is an unfinished book because an answer is missing. An answer I hope someone in the world will provide. You? (*HS* 8)

Macabéa, both a subject without fissures and a truncated, grotesquely charged version of Lispector's questing characters, carries their typical moves to a reductio ad absurdum.

The dramatization of the text's reception provides no relief from the tense interactions of the other participants in the narrative act. The encoded reader, source and recipient of violence, offers a particularly uncomfortable position for any real reader to occupy. Frequently addressing the reader as *vós* (the formal pronoun, now archaic), the narrator assumes various tones: ceremonious, religious, lyrical, or mocking. The narratee shares the narrator's niche of economic security and comes to the text with motives not entirely clean:

> (If the reader possesses some wealth and a comfortable life, he must step out of himself to see how the other at times can be. If he is poor, he won't be reading me because reading is superfluous for those who feel slight and permanent pangs of hunger. I function as an escape valve for the crushing life of the average bourgeoisie.) (*HS* 30)

This "coming out of oneself," not a pleasant escapism, involves a degrading identification, which the narrator wishes to force upon the narratee: "If there is any reader for this story, I want him to soak up the young woman like a mop on a wet floor. This girl is the truth I wished to avoid'' (*HS* 39). In another passage, the aggression against the encoded reader reaches a shriller pitch: ''Let those who read me, then, feel a punch in the stomach to see if they like it. Life is a punch in the stomach'' (*HS* 82-83). As a perpetrator of violence, the ''you'' collaborates with the forces that crush Macabéa and the narrator: ''I have to ask, though I don't know who to ask, if I must really love whoever slaughters me and ask who among you is slaughtering me'' (*HS* 81). The narratee, then, provides a fictional space for participation in the main activities figured in the text: repulsion and identification, violence, and the reception of violence. Reading the victim, like writing the victim, entails a symbolic engagement with the pressures of her life. That engagement is doubly uncomfortable, doubly suspect, in the role this text proposes for the reader: sympathy slides into suffering, and disengagement into the wielding of a malevolent power.

In her dramatization of the production, transmission, and reception of a fictional text that attempts to write the victim, Lispector allows none of the dramatic personae of author, narrator, character, and reader to occupy a comfortable position. With hyperbole and uncompromising detail, Lispector stresses the particular agencies of that victimization. Macabéa, as we have seen, is not simply a victim of social circumstances. The novella presses this point in the implicit contrast between Macabéa and her two false friends. Olímpico, also a displaced migrant from the Northeast, displays will and an evil forcefulness. Glória, a sensuous female, combines vigor with a smug self-satisfaction. Macabéa's position as a victim transcends motivations of gender, class, and what might be loosely called race, factors that nevertheless contribute to her oppression. This hyperbolically naive, unprotected, bewildered young woman—''adrift in the unconquerable city'' (*HS* 80)—signifies the shared human helplessness of beings engulfed in the brutality of life, ''life which devours life'' (*HS* 84).

Macabéa's hunger is both a product of material deprivation and a metaphor of that totally vulnerable and denuded existence that Lispector sets up as an ideal in many texts. In this polyvalent encoding of poverty, Lispector questions the dubious moral and psychic forces at work in the representation of oppression. She points up the absurd hubris of the well-off writer who imagines the position of someone who goes hungry, stressing—and giving in to—the urge to engage in just such an act of the imagination. For a writer in a city crowded with the poor, perhaps especially for a woman writer who enters into daily, intimate contact with attenuated poverty in the person of the domestic servant (I think here of the many maids, shadowy or acerbic presences, in Lispector texts), the compulsion to write the victim is in no way innocent or simple:

> In a street of Rio de Janeiro I caught a glimpse of utter disaster in the face of a young woman from the Northeast. (*HS* 12)

Care for her, ladies and gentlemen, because my power is only to show her so that you will recognize her in the street, stepping lightly because of her fluttering thinness. (*HS* 19)

These initially simple, lyrical acts of seeing, showing, and recognizing quickly absorb violent energies, as Lispector implicates—melodramatically, even histrionically, both in the misfortunes of the victim and in the powers that crush her— all the subjects who engage in the narrative transaction.

One may question whether the construction of Macabéa as both social and existential victim may not overload the circuits and disrupt any effective social criticism. A character whose "wisdom" consists of meek acceptance—"Things are the way they are because that's the way they are" (*HS* 26)—is written by a narrator who agrees with her: "Could there possibly be another answer? If someone knows a better one let him speak up for I have been waiting for years" (*HS* 26). In the preface, the "real author" echoes this statement, placing the burden of an answer on someone else. Yet if we read this novella in the context of the three stories about rape that soften the implications of sexual assault and women's oppression, we see that the very refusal to provide answers underlies the disturbing effectiveness of *The Hour of the Star*. Macabéa dies in utter abjection, learning nothing from her trials. The narrator finds no moral in his tale, and with reluctance and relief detaches himself from her in the end. Lispector refuses to naturalize the oppression of one class, or gender, or race by another, or for that matter, to see human life in heroic terms.

We might also read this novella as a parable on the motivations of narrative and on Lispector's own creative process. Peter Brooks, in *Reading for the Plot*, affirms his belief that "narrative has something to do with time boundedness, and that plot is the internal logic of the discourse of mortality":

Walter Benjamin has made this point in the simplest and most extreme way, claiming that what we seek in narrative fictions is that knowledge of death which is denied to us in our own lives: the death that writes *finis* to the life and therefore confers on it its meaning. "Death," says Benjamin, "is the sanction of everything that the story teller can tell." (Brooks 1986, 220)

A similar view about the generative connection between death and narrative drives the plot and perhaps also other instances of textual violence in *The Hour of the Star*. The narrator seems to engage, through Macabéa, in a kind of sacrificial rite, which culminates in the killing off of the protagonist. "Death is my favorite character in this story" (*HS* 83), he says. In the ritual performed by the narrative, symbolic self-immolation plays a part. The narrator remarks in one of his more histrionic moments: "I want to be a pig and a chicken, then kill them and drink their blood" (*HS* 70). Macabéa dies in a slow-motion scene that takes up seven pages. The narrator watches her suffer, gloating strangely over his power to save or kill her. He decides she must die, yet acknowledges her death as his betrayal of her. "Even you, Brutus?!" (*HS* 84), he says to himself. He claims to accompany her at the moment of dying: "Don't be afraid, death happens in an instant and is quickly over. I know because I just died with the young woman" (*HS* 85). Although in Lispector's fiction the ritual sacrifices, the charged commerce between victimizer and victim, narrator and double, do not bring about enduring illumination, much less result in dramatic change, they are essential acts that set her narratives in motion.

The Hour of the Star offers, then, a lucid representation of the aggressive investments narrative entails. Violence is no longer limited, as it was in Lispector's earlier fiction, to intrapsychic conflicts, clashes between characters, or the mimesis of social forces. Violence is no longer justified, contained, and subdued by ideological and narrative strategies. Instead, in this text and elsewhere in her fiction, the act of narration itself appears problematic, aggressive, guilt-provoking. A textual violence permeates the vertiginous doublings and mirrorings in which author, narrators, characters, and readers engage. To tell stories, for Lispector, is to give up the very possibility of innocence and to enact a knowing, guilt-ridden struggle with the mastering and violent powers of narrative.

Afterword: The Violence of a Heart

In 1952, Lispector published a *crônica* about Virginia Woolf, which, because it brings together female gender, writing, and violence, can lead us to some brief concluding thoughts (Lispector 1952b). Entitled "The Violence of a Heart" ("A violência de um coração"), Lispector's essay is a retelling of the famous Judith Shakespeare episode from Woolf's *Room of One's Own*, ending with the equally famous quotation: "Who can measure the heat and violence of the poet's heart when caught and tangled in a woman's body?" (Woolf 1929, 50). Many years later, in 1977, Lispector republished this same piece. Although reissuing something published earlier was, as we have seen, a common practice for her, it is worth speculating on her interest in this fragment of Woolf's at both the beginning and end of her career.

In 1952, Lispector was the author of three novels and one collection of short stories, already well launched as a writer. In October 1977, a few weeks before publication of *The Hour of the Star*, and less than two months before her death, she was an eminent and much fêted author in Brazil. At both these times, nevertheless, the Judith Shakespeare episode, a tragic tale of female gender laying waste a writer's talent, seemed to her worth retelling, framed as a rendition of circumstances that prevailed long ago: Virginia Woolf, "wanting to prove that no woman, in Shakespeare's time, could have written Shakespeare's plays, invented for him a sister named Judith." Perhaps the most striking aspect of Lispector's text is how closely in tone and details, although in summary form, it sticks to Woolf's plot, which contrasts William's and Judith's stories. As she narrates the fate of this imaginary sister, who, possessing talent and drive equal to her brother's, "by nature's delicate decree had been born a woman," Lispector does not elaborate or explain why this story should prove resonant for her or for her readers. Whether Lispector's implicit message is that things have changed drastically, or not enough, remains intriguingly open to interpretation. It is telling that Lispector takes up Woolf's plots and characters, not Woolf's analytical elaboration of their illustrative value. Lispector's imagination was drawn to the embodiment and lived consequences of the problem, not to its intellectual dissection. For Lispector the retold episode sufficed, leaving the reader with unanswered questions.

Why, indeed, would she have wanted to tell and retell it? A plausible answer is that, for Lispector herself, the conjunction of a poet's heart and a woman's body had an equally vivid and enduring fascination, and for her too it produced a violence tracked by many of her fictions. The targets and effects of that violence vary widely throughout her novels and short stories. A woman artist, like Joana in Lispector's first novel, may abandon gender roles, altering along the way traditional novelistic plots and character development. The interposition of a woman's body may also be a source of positive creative energy that, as in *The Stream of Life*, challenges the demarcations of autobiography and fiction, or that, as in *The Stations of the Body*, parodies and disrupts both the commonplaces of popular fiction and the complacency of narratives (her own included) that align themselves with high art. Or the writer may take up fictive residence in a man's body, telling the story through a male narrator, as in *The Hour of the Star*, to point up the complicities of narrative itself in violent structures of domination. Preceding as she did the second wave of feminism in the 1970s, which became prevalent in Brazil only in the 1980s, Lispector did not draw on the cultural discourses of feminism to gloss the Virginia Woolf passage, or to think in more explicit detail about her own writing. To do so now opens up, as I hope to have shown, a profitable route to interpreting her work. It is important to remember, however, that what we may loosely call Lispector's feminism—her concern with the predicaments of women's lives and the powers to which they have access—is never cast as a simple defense of women and the feminine, but rather as a keen awareness of the struggles in which they are active, and not necessarily morally superior, participants. In Lispector, women's hearts are not quelled and subdued, but generate heat and violence that affect the representational world of her fiction as well as the forms those fictions take.

Although it seems clear to me that aggressive forces shape much of Lispector's writing, I have often wondered whether it was appropriate to use the term "violence" metaphorically to refer to the structures of domination and victimization that I attempt to bring out. Her work does not thematize the literal, political violence of war and torture, or other overt forms of state brutality, which are all too prevalent in Latin America and indeed the world. There are crimes in Lispector, but they are used mainly for their symbolic value, as vehicles and correlatives of guilt and inner conflicts. We can see this in the jumbling of the serious and the trivial, and in the incommensurateness of the malevolent acts and their paltry objects that define some of the "crimes" in Lispector's fiction: "homicide of a wife, murder of insects, small killing of an ant, massacre of chickens and chick, involuntary killing of fish, abandonment of dog and old lady, or finally, the killing of characters" (Varin 1990, 170). The witty enumeration is Claire Varin's, but the dramatic augmentation and the devastating psychological repercussions of the seemingly trivial that its wording implies are very much in keeping with the climate of Lispector's fiction.

When compared with brutal forms of social violence, the violences in Lispector may seem tenuous, cerebral, or abstract. Yet, when Lispector turned to broader social themes in her later work, she produced memorable and scathingly effective critiques. In *Death without Weeping: The Violence of Everyday Life in Brazil*, a recent anthropological study of the overlapping forces that cause and maintain the poverty of shantytown dwellers in Northeastern Brazil, Nancy Scheper-Hughes draws an impressively detailed and vast panorama of violence suffered and practiced that dwarf any in Lispector's fiction. Yet, in attempting to bring home the negligence and bad faith of medical workers who too often prescribe expensive medicines to people weak from hunger, Scheper-Hughes finds no more telling illustration than a passage from *The Hour of the Star*: Macabéa's visit to a doctor who, despite being aware that poverty is the cause of her malnutrition, finds it more convenient to suspect a neurosis and advises her to see a psychiatrist.

I retained, finally, the term "violence," in part because Lispector herself found it resonant and necessary and in part because of the connections it implies between the psychic and the social, connections that Lispector's later work increasingly addressed. If the violence of patriarchy is thematized from the beginning, it is only slowly that her fiction comes to incorporate other kinds of social violence perpetrated by the class system and the political order, and to foreground and question the violence of narrative itself. The forces of oppression, and the violence of their action and reaction, are no longer directed against or located mainly in women's hearts and bodies, but are mapped in their multiple social and narrative sites. The term "violence" is, then, intended to point up the extent to which Lispector became an acute and unsparing observer of even the subtlest and least conspicuous forms that violence can take, and, as her work progressed, an increasingly aware witness to the interconnection between private and public kinds of violence, including the complex ways in which they implicate writers and readers.

Notes

Introduction

I use the following abbreviations for Lispector's works cited frequently throughout the book. The dates are those of the English translations.

DW: *Discovering the World* (Lispector 1992)

FL: *The Foreign Legion* (Lispector 1986)

FT: *Family Ties* (Lispector 1972)

HS: *The Hour of the Star* (Lispector 1986)

SB: *The Stations of the Body* (Lispector 1989)

SL: *The Stream of Life* (Lispector 1989)

WH: *Near to the Wild Heart* (Lispector 1990)

Page numbers follow the abbreviations and refer to the published English translations, although I often modify them for reasons of accuracy or to retain shades of meaning that are important to my interpretations.

Translations from Portuguese, French, and Spanish of quotations from interviews, letters, articles, and books, unless otherwise noted, are my own.

1. This account, in an interview with Lispector's family members and friends after her death, is by Tania Kauffman, Lispector's sister.

2. In one interview, Lispector emphasized that both male and female writers imitated her work, and in another maintained that "it just happened" that the sole character of her novel *The Passion according to G.H.* was female, as if wanting to escape any restriction, either of her influence or of her fictional imagination, along gender lines (Gilio 1976, 44; Lapouge and Pisa

1977, 198). Yet, in another interview, she stated proudly that she was "a pioneer of female journalism in Brazil. At the time [1940-43, approximately], I was the only woman working on the newspaper" (Lowe 1979, 37).

3. Claire Varin's two books (1987, 1990), the first a translation of selections from several interviews with Lispector and the second a critical interpretation of Lispector's biography and texts, contain the most reliable biographical information available on Lispector, based on archival research and interviews with her sisters (one of whom has since died) and other family members and friends.

4. Clarice Lispector Archive in the Arquivo-Museu de Literatura (Archival Museum of Literature), Fundação Casa de Rui Barbosa, Rio de Janeiro. The material in this archive was donated by Lispector's son Paulo Gurgel Valente in two stages, the first in 1977 and the second a few years later. For a description of the contents of this archive, see Vasconcellos (1993).

5. Nelson Vieira has studied Jewish myths and motifs in Lispector's fiction. (See Vieira 1987.)

6. Clippings from this section in the Rio daily *Correio da Manhã* dated from August 1959 to October 1960, including some typescript drafts corrected in Lispector's hand, are in the Clarice Lispector Archive.

7. This was corroborated by her son Paulo Gurgel Valente, who said that after the accident, which occurred in the early morning hours of September 14, 1967, she became very depressed and closed herself off from people. "She was vain. Her physical appearance, her image mattered very much to her" (Moreira 1981).

1. The Young Artist and the Snares of Gender

1. See, for instance, the interview with Colasanti, Salgueiro, and Sant'Anna (October 20, 1976), where, in answer to the interviewer's surmise that she must have been a girl of seventeen or eighteen when she published *Near to the Wild Heart* Lispector says, "Yes. I was seventeen" (Colasanti et al. 1988, 298).

2. What I take to be her actual birth date is on several I.D. cards and on her registration as a Brazilian citizen; the later dates are on two curricula vitae she prepared toward the end of her life (Clarice Lispector Archive).

3. This sentence is inexplicably omitted from the English translation, but should have appeared, along with a few other missing words, before the last line of page 48. Page numbers refer to Giovanni Pontiero's translation of *Near to the Wild Heart* (Lispector 1990), henceforth abbreviated *WH* and cited in the text.

4. Hélène Cixous considers this novel a portrait of the artist but is interested mainly in the implications of the initial father-daughter alliance and especially in Joana's maternal father. See the three-page section, "The Mother Father of the Artist" in "Reaching the Point of Wheat" (Cixous 1987b), and "Writing and the Law: Blanchot, Joyce, Kafka, and Lispector" (Cixous 1991b). Two other recent readings consider the novel from a feminist perspective, although not as a *Künstlerroman*. Cristina Ferreira Pinto (1990) analyzes the novel as a *Bildungsroman*, and Ellen Douglass (1990) sees the novel as the first of Lispector's many critiques and revisions of the patriarchal structure of the quest.

5. The English translation is unaccountably inaccurate in some passages, offering what amounts to revisions of Lispector's text. For instance, Pontiero's translation of the passage just quoted omits the figurative castration, restoring to the teacher the power Lispector curtails: "The teacher was like a great tom-cat reigning supreme in a cellar" (*WH* 105). As is the case here, some of the inaccuracies reflect issues of gender. Pontiero retitles Lispector's chapter "The Mother" as "One Day"; another chapter, "The Departure of the Men" (Lispector), becomes "the Man's Departure."

6. Benedito Nunes (1973, 87). His brief discussion of this story (84-87) is the only critical commentary on it that I have seen.

7. References to *The Foreign Legion* refer to Pontiero's translation (Lispector 1986), abbreviated *FL* and cited in the text.

2. Female Power in *Family Ties*

1. Quotations from *Family Ties* refer to Pontiero's translation (Lispector 1972), abbreviated *FT* and cited in the text.

2. This chapter is a revised and expanded version of "*Family Ties*: Female Development in Clarice Lispector," an essay that appeared in Abel, Hirsch, and Langland (1983, 287-303).

3. Clarice Lispector, *Alguns contos*, 1952. The collection contains, in this sequence: "Mystery in São Cristóvão," "Family Ties," "Beginnings of a Fortune," "Love," "A Chicken," and "The Dinner."

4. A letter from the Brazilian novelist Fernando Sabino dated March 30, 1955, gives his response to eight stories Lispector had sent him. Of these, four were included later in *Family Ties*: "The Imitation of the Rose," "The Daydreams of a Drunk Woman," "Happy Birthday," and "The Crime of the Mathematics Teacher." Sabino's response was fervently positive: "You have written eight stories as no one even remotely has been able to write in Brazil. You are writing like no one—saying what no one dared to say" (Clarice Lispector Archive).

5. Roberto Corrêa dos Santos's excellent analysis (1986, 45-57), the only discussion of this story I have seen, does not consider questions of gender.

6. Although page numbers in the text refer to the Pontiero translation, in my revision of it here I sometimes borrow from Elizabeth Bishop's excellent English version of "The Smallest Woman in the World" in Barbara Howes's anthology (1973, 320-28).

3. The Nurturing Text in Hélène Cixous and Clarice Lispector

1. There is some overlap in the contents of these books. *Vivre l'orange/To Live the Orange* is reprinted in *L'heure de Clarice Lispector* (1989), which includes two other essays. *Reading with Clarice Lispector* (1990) is not a book Cixous wrote for publication but a transcription and translation of seminars on Clarice Lispector that Cixous gave at the Université de Paris VII—Vincennes at Saint-Denis and at the Collège Internationale de Philosophie between 1980 and 1985.

2. *Vivre l'orange/To live the Orange* (Cixous 1979b, 10). Hereafter, when cited in the text, it will be abbreviated *TLO*.

3. Cixous's 1979 essay, which appeared in *Poétique*, came out in English as "Clarice Lispector: The Approach, Letting Oneself (be) Read (by) Clarice Lispector, The Passion According to C.L." (Cixous 1991a, 59-77). Hereafter, when cited in the text, it will be abbreviated CLA.

4. "Reaching the Point of Wheat" (Cixous 1987b); hereafter, when cited in the text, it will be abbreviated RPW.

5. "Extrême fidélité" came out in French in the Brazilian periodical *Travessia* (Cixous 1987a), in an issue honoring the tenth anniversary of Lispector's death. A somewhat modified version of the same text later appeared in France as "L'auteur en verité" ("The Author in Truth") in *L'heure de Clarice Lispector* (Cixous 1989) and later in English (Cixous 1991a). I will quote most often from the English translation, which hereafter, when cited in the text will be abbreviated AT.

6. I occasionally modify this translation, cited in the text and abbreviated *FL*.

7. I am aware that Cixous denies this pointedly, as for instance, in this excerpt from an interview conducted in 1984: "I do not care to master a text. I am not interested in that. I am not interested in

making it enter into categories, because really I grant myself the luxury to read in texts only that which for me is a question of life and death'' (Conley 1991, 153).

8. I am indebted to Anna Klobucka, in conversation and in her outline for a graduate seminar paper, for the idea of placing *The Hour of the Star* as Lispector's "answer" to the dilemma of the approach to the other that engages Cixous in her reading of Lispector.

4. A Woman Writing: Fiction and Autobiography in *The Stream of Life* and *Stations of the Body*

1. Quotations from *The Stream of Life* refer to the English translation (Lispector 1989), abbreviated *SL* and cited in the text.

2. This draft is available for consultation in the Clarice Lispector Archive. Alexandrino Severino (1989) compares the published *Stream of Life* with an even earlier version written in 1971 and given to him by Lispector herself for translation. "This first version had the title ''Behind Thinking: A Dialogue with Life,'' but was later called ''Screaming Object,'' or simply ''Object'' (Severino 1988, 116). This earlier version, if not identical, must have been close to the draft in the Clarice Lispector Archive because Severino observes that the typescript in his possession differs from the published version ''mainly regarding the inclusion of biographical aspects'' (Severino 1988, 116). The thrust of Severino's article is to justify Lispector's revisions as aesthetic improvements.

3. The other typescript, also at the Clarice Lispector Archive, is of a collection of short stories she wrote between 1940 and 1941, organized by Lispector but left unpublished at her death. It was posthumously published with Lispector's last two short stories under the title *A bela e a fera* (*The Beauty and the Beast*) (Lispector 1979). Benedito Nunes has reprinted the facsimile of the manuscript of one of these last two stories, ''A bela e a fera, ou a ferida grande demais,'' accompanied by his transcriptions of Lispector's corrections, in the critical edition of *A paixão segundo G.H.* (*The Passion according to G.H.*; Lispector 1988, 117-50).

4. Most of the paragraphs or pages are crossed out with large *X*'s, even passages that appear almost verbatim in the published version, leading me to believe that the *X*'s were merely an aid to the retyping of the manuscript.

5. "Objeto gritante," p. 88, my translation. References to this draft of *The Stream of Life*, abbreviated OG, will hereafter be cited in the text.

6. A 768-page selection of these *crônicas* made by Lispector's son Paulo Gurgel Valente includes the reprints from earlier publications, but excludes *crônicas* he considered excessively circumstantial, as he explains in a prefatory note. This selection was published posthumously under the title *A descoberta do mundo* (Lispector 1984) and translated as *Discovering the World* (Lispector 1992).

7. *The Stations of the Body* met with many negative reviews when it first came out, and few critical commentaries have been written about it. Recently, two articles attempt to correct this neglect: Earl Fitz (1988a) searches for continuities between Lispector's earlier and later fiction, and Nelson Vieira (1988) emphasizes the changes in Lispector's craft. I might point out here that if in this collection Lispector has not actually written popular fiction—the autobiographical metafictional considerations complicate considerably the straightforwardness of the fictional stories—neither has she written fiction that became popular, in the sense of being widely read. The book has not reached a wide readership, to judge by the two printings it has had in Brazil to date. It has, in fact, sold far less well than the densely written *Family Ties*, now in its twenty-fourth printing.

8. That Lispector watched these soap operas is evident from the letters to her son during his semester abroad in the United States, from January to June 1969. She gives concise and comic summaries of the latest plot turns, sometimes preceded by the phrase, ''Siléia (her maid) asks me to tell you . . . '' (letters to Paulo Gurgel Valente, Clarice Lispector Archive).

9. Quotations from *The Stations of the Body* refer to the English translation (Lispector 1989), abbreviated *SB* and cited in the text.

10. The reference to Dalton Trevisan was edited out of the versions of this story Lispector published in the two 1974 short story collections. The reference to Nelson Rodrigues in the text persists in *Where You Were at Night*, but disappears in *The Stations of the Body*. In both collections the title was changed to "A Complicated Case."

11. Lispector herself often quoted these words of Flaubert in interviews. See, for instance, the 1974 interview in which she is asked: "To what extent are you Joana from *Near to the Wild Heart*, a lucid person who cannot find herself?" Clarice: "Flaubert once said: 'Madame Bovary, c'est moi' " (Varin 1987, 69).

5. Rape and Textual Violence

1. A slightly modified version of this chapter appeared in *Rape and Representation* (Higgins and Silver 1991).

2. I modify here Laura Mulvey's sharp formulation, "Sadism demands a story," quoted and discussed in its possible reversibility by Teresa de Lauretis: "Is a story, are all stories to be claimed by sadism?" (de Lauretis 1982, 102).

3. Quotations from *The Hour of the Star* refer to the English translation (Lispector 1986b), abbreviated *HS* and cited in the text.

4. The Brazilian film *The Hour of the Star* (1986), directed by Suzana Amaral and available in the United States, is a very interesting adaptation of Lispector's novella. Considerably less corrosive than its literary counterpart, the film stresses the failed Cinderella plot and (wisely) omits the mediated narration and metafictional meditations.

Bibliography

Abel, Elizabeth, Marianne Hirsch, and Elizabeth Langland, eds. 1983. *The Voyage In: Fictions of Female Development*. Hanover: University Press of New England.
Ambruster, Carol. 1983. Hélène-Clarice: Nouvelle voix. *Contemporary Literature* 24 (2): 145-57.
Benjamin, Jessica. 1988. *The Bonds of Love: Psychoanalysis, Feminism, and the Problem of Domination*. New York: Pantheon Books.
Bakhtin, Mikhail. 1968. *Rabelais and His World*. Trans. Helen Iswolski. Cambridge: M.I.T. Press.
Becherucci, Bruna. 1974. Lixo, sim. *Veja*, 31 de julho.
Borelli, Olga. 1981. *Clarice Lispector: Esboço para um possível retrato*. Rio de Janeiro: Nova Fronteira.
Borges, Jorge Luis. 1944. *Ficciones*. Buenos Aires: Sur.
Brooks, Peter. 1985. *The Melodramatic Imagination: Balzac, Henry James, Melodrama and the Mode of Excess*. 2d ed. New York: Columbia University Press.
———. 1986. *Reading for the Plot: Design and Intention in Narrative*. New York: Knopf.
Cixous, Hélène. 1973. *Portrait du soleil*. Paris: Denoel.
———. 1979a. L'approche de Clarice Lispector, Se laisser lire (par) Clarice Lispector, A paixão segundo CL. *Poétique* 40: 408-19.
———. 1979b. *Vivre l'orange/To live the Orange*. (English text by Cixous based on a translation by Ann Liddle and Sarah Cornell.) Paris: des femmes.
———. 1987a. Extrême fidélité. *Travessia* 14:11-45.
———. 1987b. Reaching the Point of Wheat, or a Portrait of the Artist as a Maturing Woman. *New Literary History* 19 (1): 1-21.
———. 1989. *L'heure de Clarice Lispector*. Paris: des femmes.
———. 1990. *Reading with Clarice Lispector*. Minneapolis: University of Minnesota Press.
———. 1991a. *"Coming to Writing" and Other Essays*. Cambridge: Harvard University Press.
———. 1991b. *Readings: The Poetics of Blanchot, Joyce, Kafka, Kleist, Lispector, and Tsvetayeva*. Minneapolis: University of Minnesota Press.
Colasanti, Marina, João Salgueiro, and Affonso Romano de Sant'Anna. 1988. October 20, 1976 in-

terview with Clarice Lispector for the Museum of Image and Sound in Rio de Janeiro. Excerpted in *A paixão segundo G.H.*, ed. Benedito Nunes. Coleção Arquivo. Florianópolis: Universidade Federal de Santa Catarina.

Conley, Verena Andermatt. 1984. Appendix: An exchange with Hélène Cixous (January 1982 interview). In *Hélène Cixous: Writing the Feminine*. Lincoln: University of Nebraska Press.

──────. 1991. Introduction. In *Readings: The Poetics of Blanchot, Joyce, Kafka, Kleist, Lispector, and Tsvetayeva* by Hélène Cixous. Minneapolis: University of Minnesota Press.

de Lauretis, Teresa. 1984. Desire in Narrative. In *Alice Doesn't: Feminism, Semiotics, Cinema*. Bloomington: Indiana University Press.

Douglass, Ellen. 1990. Female Quest toward "Água Pura" in Clarice Lispector's *Perto do Coração Selvagem*. *Brasil/Brazil* 3 (3): 45-61.

DuPlessis, Rachel Blau. 1985. *Writing beyond the Ending: Narrative Strategies of Twentieth-century Women Writers*. Bloomington: Indiana University Press.

Fitz, Earl. 1985. *Clarice Lispector*. Boston: Twayne.

──────. 1987. A Discourse of Silence: The Postmodernism of Clarice Lispector. *Contemporary Literature* 28 (4): 420-26.

──────. 1988a. A Writer in Transition: Clarice Lispector and *A Via Crucis do Corpo*. *Latin American Literary Review* 16 (32): 41-52.

──────. 1988b. The Passion of Logo (centrism), or, The Deconstructionist Universe of Clarice Lispector. *Luso-Brazilian Review* 25 (2): 34-44.

Gilio, María Ester. 1976. Tristes trópicos (interview with Clarice Lispector). *Crisis* 4 (39): 43-45.

Gorga Filho, Remy. 1969. A admirável autora de *Laços de família* não é um mito. *Correio do Povo* (Porto Alegre), March 15.

Gotlib, Nádia Battella. 1988. Um fio de voz: histórias de Clarice. In Clarice Lispector, *A paixão segundo G.H.*, ed. Benedito Nunes. Coleção Arquivos. Florianópolis: Universidade Federal de Santa Catarina.

Herrmann, Claudine. 1980. The Virile System. In *New French Feminisms*, eds. Elaine Marks and Isabelle de Courtivron. Amherst: University of Massachussetts Press.

Hertz, Neil. 1985. Recognizing Causabon. In *End of the Line: Essays on Pychoanalysis and the Sublime*. New York: Columbia University Press.

Higgins, Lynn, and Brenda Silver, eds. 1991. *Rape and Representation*. New York: Columbia University Press.

Hill, Amariles G. 1976. A experiência de existir narrando. In *Seleta de Clarice Lispector*, eds. Renato C. Gomes and Amariles G. Hill. Rio de Janeiro: José Olympio.

Howes, Barbara, ed. 1973. *The Eye of the Heart: Short Stories from Latin America*. New York: Bobbs-Merrill.

Jackson, K. David, ed. 1987. *Transformations of Literary Language in Latin American Literature: From Machado de Assis to the Vanguards*. Austin: Department of Spanish and Portuguese, University of Texas at Austin/Abaporu Press.

Jones, Ann Rosalind. 1985. Inscribing Femininity: French Theories of the Feminine. In *Making a Difference: Feminist Literary Criticism*, eds. Gail Green and Coppélia Kahn. New York: Methuen.

Kristeva, Julia. 1986. Stabat mater, trans. Léon S. Roudiez. In *The Kristeva Reader*, ed. Toril Moi. New York: Columbia University Press.

Lamare, Germana de. 1972. Clarice Lispector esconde um objeto gritante. *Correio da Manhã* (Rio de Janeiro), March 6.

Laplanche, J., and J. B. Pontalis. 1973. *The Language of Psychoanalysis*. Trans. Donald Nicholson-Smith. New York: Norton.

Lapouge, Maryvonne, and Clelia Pisa, eds. 1977. *Brasileiras: voix, écrits du Brésil*. Paris: des femmes.

Lindstrom, Naomi. A Discourse Analysis of "Preciosidade" by Clarice Lispector. *Luso-Brazilian Review* 12 (2): 187-94.

Lins, Álvaro. 1963. A experiência incompleta: Clarice Lispector. In *Os mortos de sobrecasaca*. Rio de Janeiro: Civilização Brasileira.

Lispector, Clarice. 1944. *Perto do coração selvagem*. Rio de Janeiro: A Noite.

———. 1952a. *Alguns contos*. Rio de Janeiro: Ministério de Educação e Saúde.

———. 1952b. A violência de um coração. *Comício*. (Also published in a Rio de Janeiro newspaper I have not been able to identify, dated October 29 and 30, 1977. Photocopy in Clarice Lispector Archive.)

———. 1960. *Laços de família*. Rio de Janeiro: Francisco Alves.

———. 1961. *A maçã no escuro*. Rio de Janeiro: Francisco Alves.

———. 1964. *A legião estrangeira*. Rio de Janeiro: Editora do Autor.

———. 1964. *A paixão segundo G.H.* Rio de Janeiro: Editora do Autor. Critical edition, 1988, ed. Benedito Nunes. Coleção Arquivos. Florianópolis: Universidade Federal de Santa Catarina.

———. 1967. *The Apple in the Dark (A maçã no escuro)*. Trans. Gregory Rabassa. New York: Knopf.

———. 1971. *Felicidade clandestina*. Rio de Janeiro: Sabiá.

———. 1972. *Family Ties (Laços de família)*. Trans. Giovanni Pontiero. Austin: University of Texas Press.

———. 1973. *Água viva*. Rio de Janeiro: Artenova.

———. 1974a. *Onde estivestes de noite*. Rio de Janeiro: Artenova.

———. 1974b. *A via crucis do corpo*. Rio de Janeiro: Artenova.

———. 1975. *De corpo inteiro*. Rio de Janeiro: Artenova.

———. 1977. *A hora da estrela*. Rio de Janeiro: José Olympio.

———. 1978. *Um sopro de vida*. Rio de Janeiro: Nova Fronteira.

———. 1979. *A bela e a fera*. Rio de Janeiro: Nova Fronteira.

———. 1984. *A descoberta do mundo*. Rio de Janeiro: Nova Fronteira.

———. 1986a. *The Foreign Legion: Stories and Chronicles (A legião estrangeira)*. Trans. Giovanni Pontiero. Manchester: Carcanet.

———. 1986b. *The Hour of the Star (A hora da estrela)*. Trans. Giovanni Pontiero. Manchester: Carcanet.

———. 1988. *The Passion according to G.H. (A paixão segundo G.H.)*. Trans. Ronald W. Sousa. Minneapolis: University of Minnesota Press.

———. 1989. *Soulstorm* (contains *Where You Were at Night* and *The Stations of the Body*; *Onde estivestes de noite* and *A via crucis do corpo*). Trans. Alexis Levitin. New York: New Directions.

———. 1990. *Near to the Wild Heart (Perto do coração selvagem)*. Trans. Giovanni Pontiero. New York: New Directions.

———. 1992. *Discovering the World (A descoberta do mundo)*. Trans. Giovanni Pontiero. Manchester: Carcanet.

———. Clarice Lispector Archive. In the Arquivo-Museu de Literatura da Fundação Casa Rui Barbosa, Rio de Janeiro.

Lispector, Elisa. 1948. *No exílio*. 2d. ed. 1971. (1st ed. 1948.) Brasília: Ebrasa/Instituto Nacional do Livro.

Lowe, Elizabeth. 1979. The Passion according to C. L. (1976 interview with Clarice Lispector). *Review* 24: 34-37.

Melo Neto, João Cabral de. 1975. *Poesias Completos*. Rio de Janeiro: José Olympio.

Moers, Ellen. 1976. *Literary Women: The Great Writers*. New York: Doubleday.

Moi, Toril. 1985. Hélène Cixous: An Imaginary Utopia. In *Sexual/Textual Politics*. New York: Methuen.

Moreira, Virgílio Moretzshon. 1981. Mil dias sem Clarice. *Manchete* (February 14).

Nunes, Benedito. 1966. *O Mundo de Clarice Lispector*. Manaus: Edições do Governo do Estado de Amazonas.
———. 1973. *Leitura de Clarice Lispector*. São Paulo: Quíron, 1973.
———. 1982. Clarice Lispector ou o naufrágio da introspecção. *Colóquio/Letras* 70:13-22.
———. 1988. Nota filológica. In *A paixão segundo G.H.*, ed. Benedito Nunes. Coleção Arquivos. Florianópolis: Editora da Universidade Federal de Santa Catarina.
Pessanha, José Américo Motta. 1965. Itinerário da paixão. *Cadernos Brasileiros* 7 (29): 63-76.
Pinto, Cristina Ferreira. 1990. *Perto do coração selvagem*: Romance de formação, romance de transformação. In *O Bildungsroman feminino: Quatro exemplos brasileiros*. São Paulo: Perspectiva.
Pizarnik, Alejandra. 1968. *Extracción de la piedra de locura*. Buenos Aires: Editorial Sudamericana.
Rich, Adrienne. 1979. Vesuvius at Home: The Power of Emily Dickinson. In *On Lies, Secrets, and Silence: Selected Prose 1966-1978*. New York: Norton.
Rodrigues, Nelson. 1961. *100 contos escolhidos: A vida como ela é*. 2 vols. Rio de Janeiro: J. Ozon. Editor.
Rodríguez Monegal, Emir. 1966. The Contemporary Brazilian Novel. *Daedalus* 95 (4): 986-1003.
Rose, Jacqueline. 1991. *The Haunting of Sylvia Plath*. London: Virago.
Rosowski, Susan J. 1983. The Novel of Awakening. In *The Voyage In: Fictions of Female Development*, eds. Elizabeth Abel, Marianne Hirsch, and Elizabeth Langland. Hanover: University Press of New England.
Sá, Olga de. 1979. *A escritura de Clarice Lispector*. Petrópolis: Vozes.
Sant'Anna, Affonso Romano. 1973. *Laços de família* e *Legião estrangeira*. In *Análise estrutural de romances brasileiros*. Petrópolis: Vozes.
Santos, Roberto Correa dos. 1986. *Clarice Lispector*. São Paulo: Atual.
———. 1990. Artes de fiandeira. Introduction to Clarice Lispector, *Laços de família*, 20th ed. Rio de Janeiro: Francisco Alves.
Scheper-Hughes, Nancy. 1992. *Death without Weeping: The Violence of Everyday Life in Brazil*. Berkeley: University of California Press.
Schwarz, Roberto. 1965. Perto do coração selvagem. In *A sereia e o desconfiado: Ensaios críticos*. Rio de Janeiro: Civilização Brasileira.
Severino, Alexandrino. 1989. As duas versões de *Água viva*. *Remate de Males* 9:115-18.
Shiach, Morag. 1991. *Hélène Cixous: A Poetics of Writing*. London: Routledge.
Spivak, Gayatri C. 1981. French Feminism in an International Frame. *Yale French Studies* 62: 154-84.
Stanton, Domna C. 1986. Difference on Trial: A Critique of the Maternal Metaphor in Cixous, Irigaray, and Kristeva. In *The Poetics of Gender*, ed. Nancy K. Miller. New York: Columbia University Press.
Suleiman, Susan Rubin. 1991. Writing Past the Wall or the Passion According to H.C. Introduction to *"Coming to Writing" and Other Essays* by Hélène Cixous. Cambridge: Harvard University Press.
Varin, Claire. 1987. *Clarice Lispector: Rencontres Brésiliennes*. Québec: Trois.
———. 1990. *Langues de feu: essais sur Clarice Lispector*. Québec: Trois.
Vasconcellos, Eliane. 1993. O arquivo de Clarice Lispector. *Quadrant* 93.
Vieira, Nelson. 1987. A linguagem espiritual de Clarice Lispector. *Travessia* 14: 81-93.
———. 1988. The Stations of the Body: Clarice Lispector's "Abertura" and Renewal. *Studies in Short Fiction* 26 (1): 55-69.
Waldman, Berta. 1983. *Clarice Lispector*. São Paulo: Brasiliense.
Woolf, Virginia. 1929. *A Room of One's Own*. New York: Harcourt Brace Jovanovich.
Yaeger, Patricia. 1989. Toward a Female Sublime. In *Gender and Theory*, ed. Linda Kauffman. Oxford: Blackwell.

Index

Compiled by Mary Rasmussen

About Chinese Women, 45
age, 32
Apple in the Dark, An (A maçã no escuro), xvii, 44
"Author in Truth, The," 51, 58

Bakhtin, Mikhail, 94
Balzac, Honoré de, 26
Barthes, Roland, 66
Becherucci, Bruna, 61
"Before the Law" (Kafka), 50
"Beginnings of a Fortune, The" (*Family Ties*), 26
Benjamin, Jessica, xiii-xiv
Benjamin, Walter, 98
Bergman, Ingmar, 45
betrayal, 34
"Body, The" (*The Stations of the Body*), 73
Borelli, Olga, xvi-xvii
Braga, Rubem, 35-36
Breath of Life, A (Um sopro de vida), xiii, xx
Brooks, Peter, 26, 90, 98
"Buffalo, The" (*Family Ties*), 29-31, 33-34

"Chicken, A" (*Family Ties*), 36
chickens, 36, 53-58
Chien andalou, Le, 21

Cixous, Hélène, xii, xviii-xix, 6, 39-59; autobiography, 42-45, 48; critical strategy, 47-48, 51-52; fictional presentation of Lispector, 43-44; intersubjective relations, 39, 41; Portuguese language, 47-49
Clarice Lispector (Fitz), xix
"Clarice Lispector: The Approach," 42, 46, 48
Colasanti, Marina, xvii
Comtesse de Ségur. See Rostopchine, Sophie
Conley, Verena Andermatt, 46, 53
"Crime of the Mathematics Teacher, The" (*Family Ties*), 34

"Day by Day" (*The Stations of the Body*), 73, 76
"Daydreams of a Drunk Woman, The" (*Family Ties*), 24
De corpo inteiro, 66
de Lauretis, Teresa, xiii-xiv, 5
"Dinner, The" (*Family Ties*), 34-35
domestic life, 27, 33, 37; in "Love," 28-30
DuPlessis, Rachel, 5

economy, libidinal, xii-xiii, 40, 45-47, 49-50
écriture féminine, xviii, 39-40, 42, 46, 48
"Egg and the Chicken, The" (*The Foreign Legion*), 44, 47, 53-58

"Egg and the Chicken, The: Love Is Not Having," 53
eggs, 53-58
Eliot, George, 81
evil, 2-3, 16
"Explanation" (*The Stations of the Body*), 74, 77-78, 80
"Extrême fidélité," 51-52, 58-59

"Family Ties" (*Family Ties*), 27-28; family relationships, 27
Family Ties (Laços de família), xix, 18, 24-38; gender and power, 25, 27, 32, 35-36, 38; initiation, 26-27; physical/psychological aberration, 24; victimization, 82
female sublime, 68, 71
feminine roles, 6, 22, 25, 28-29, 33, 35-36; in *Near to the Wild Heart*, 11-12, 17
feminism, xii-xiii
Fitz, Earl, xviii-xix
Fonseca, Rubem, 75-76
"For the Time Being" (*The Stations of the Body*), 73, 76
Foreign Legion, The (A legião estrangeira), xv, 18, 25, 64-65

gender, xii-xiii, xix, 17-18, 60, 71; and female talent, 2-3, 100; ideology, xiv, 88; and psychoanalysis, 25; roles, xix, 15, 21, 25, 35-36, 80, 101; and writing, 2, 3, 5, 17, 21, 22, 23, 60, 71, 72, 76, 79, 80, 92, 100, 101
Good Mother, 47, 56
Gorga Filho, Remy, xvi
Gotlib, Nádia Battella, 65

"Happy Birthday" (*Family Ties*), 29, 31-33, 53
Herrmann, Claudine, 10
Hertz, Neil, 81
Hill, Amariles G., 37
Hour of Clarice Lispector (L'heure de Clarice Lispector), 39
Hour of the Star, The (A hora da estrela), xiv, xx, 51, 58-59, 101; narrative, 91-93, 96-99; victimization, 83, 89-99
Hour of the Wolf, The, 45

"Imitation of the Rose, The" (*Family Ties*), 29-30, 33

In Exile (No exilio), xvii
intelligence, 19, 22, 62

James, Henry, 26
Jones, Ann, 45-46
Jornal do Brasil, 64-65, 75, 79
Joyce, James, xvii, 49-50

Klein, Melanie, 47
Kristeva, Julia, 5, 45, 78

Lamare, Germana de, 67
Laplanche, J., 52
Lapouge, Maryvonne, xvii
Lindstrom, Naomi, 86
Lins, Álvaro, 4
Lispector, Clarice, xi, xvi-xviii; autobiography, xiii, xv, 61, 63-66, 72-73, 76, 80; columns (*crônicas*), 64-66, 75, 79-80; commissioned stories, 72, 74-75; crisis, 26; epiphany, xviii, 18, 25, 33, 68; gender, narrative, and violence, xii-xiii, xix-xx, 99-102; gender and power, 24, 35-36, 38, 68; interviews, 66; model of feminine writings, 50; nurturing and writing, 53-58; Portuguese language, xi-xii; reading, xvii; rhetorical strategy, 19; syntax of, xii
Lispector, Elisa, xvii
"Love" (*Family Ties*), 28-30, 33
loving and writing, 2, 10, 18, 21-23
Lowe, Elizabeth, xvii
loyalty, 29

madness. *See* mental illness
Manchete, 66
manhood, 34-35
"Man Who Appeared, The" (*The Stations of the Body*), 77
marriage, 9, 15
masculine roles, 25, 33-35
matriarchy, 31-32
Melo Neto, João Cabral de, 60
mental illness, 30, 33
metaphor, 19, 26; birds, 36-37; birth, 70; cutting/killing, 32; fishing, 62; gestation, birth, and breath, 15-16; orality, 20; prison, 28, 33; train of madness, 30; voice, 12
mimesis, 74, 78, 80, 90, 92-93
"Miraculous Fishing" (*The Foreign Legion*), 19

"Misfortunes of Sofia, The" (*The Foreign Legion*), xix, 2, 18-23; destiny, 21; transgressions, 18, 23
"Miss Algrave" (*The Stations of the Body*), 73-74
Modleski, Tania, xiv
Moers, Ellen, 36
Moi, Toril, 47
Moreira, Virgílio Moretzshon, xi
motherhood, 27-28, 31-33, 38, 76-78; in *Near to the Wild Heart*, 10-11; in "The Way of the Cross," 78
Mother's Day, 76
Mulvey, Laura, xiv
"Mystery in São Cristóvão" (*Family Ties*), 26, 83-84

narration, xii-xiv, 13, 27, 51; and aggression, 16
Near to the Wild Heart (Perto do coração selvagem), xii, xix, 1, 3-18, 50; abandonment, 14-15; intellectual competition, 8-10; *Künstlerroman*, 1, 4; Oedipal structures, 5-6; poetic invention, 5; transgressions, 10; triangular configurations, 7-8, 13-14, 17; victimization, 82
Nunes, Benedito, xiv, xviii, 3-4, 54, 63-64, 80-81

Oedipus model, xiv; patterns of narrative, 70-71
oppression, 89; class prejudice, 93

Palmer, Helen, xviii
passion, xv
Passion according to G.H., The (A paixão segundo G.H.), xv, xx, 66, 82
passivity, 32-33, 36
patriarchy, 3, 72, 90; in "The Dinner," 35; in *The Stations of the Body*, 77-78
Pessanha, José Américo, 66-67
"Pig Latin" (*The Stations of the Body*), 72, 83, 87-89
Pisa, Clelia, xvii
Pizarnik, Alejandra, xi
Plath, Sylvia, 79
"Plaza Mauá" (*The Stations of the Body*), 77-78
Pontalis, J. B., 52
Portrait du Soleil, 44

Portrait of the Artist as a Young Man (Joyce), 4, 50
"Preciousness" (*Family Ties*), 26, 83-87; power, gender, and sexuality, 85
prostitution, 74, 80; in "Pig Latin," 87-88; writer as prostitute, 79
pygmies, 37-38

rape, 83-89
"Reaching the Point of Wheat, or A Portrait of the Artist as a Maturing Woman (Cixous)," 49, 51
Reading for the Plot (Brooks), 98
Reading with Clarice Lispector (Cixous), xix, 39, 42, 49
Rich, Adrienne, 14
Rodrigues, Nelson, 75-76
Rodríguez, Monegal E., xii
Rosa, João Guimaraes, xii, xviii, 4
Rose, Jacqueline, 79
Rosowski, Susan J., 28-29
Rostopchine, Sophie, 18

Sant'Anna, Affonso Romano, 25-26
Santos, Roberto Correa dos, 25-26, 34
Schwarz, Roberto, 4
"Screaming Object" ("Objeto gritante"), 63-67
"Secret Happiness" ("Felicidade Clandestina"), 54
sexuality, 72-73, 75, 77, 80; in "Mystery in São Cristóvão," 26-27; sexual respectability rules, 76
Shiach, Morag, 44
"Smallest Woman in the World, The" (*Family Ties*), 37
Spivak, Gayatri, 45-46
Stanton, Domna, 48
Stations of the Body, The (A via crucis do corpo), xx, 61, 72-81, 101
Stream of Life, The (Água viva), xx, 61-72, 81, 101
Suleiman, Susan, 41-42

To Live the Orange (Vivre l'orange), 39, 42-46, 48
Trevisan, Dalton, 75-76

Valente, Paulo Gurgel, 64
values, reversal of, 33

Varin, Claire, xvii, 67
victimization, 82-99
violence, xii-xiii, xv-xvi, 2, 17, 23, 73, 75; against women, xx, 83, 85-89
"Violence of a Heart, The" ("A violência de um coração"), 100
virginity, 78

Waldman, Berta, 4, 95

"Way of the Cross, The" (*The Stations of the Body*), 73, 78
women: nurturing, 47-48, 50; violence against, xx, 83, 85-89; and writing, xix-xx, 1-2, 10, 48, 61, 76
Woolf, Virginia, xvii, 100

Yaeger, Patricia, 68, 71

Marta Peixoto is associate professor of Portuguese at New York University. She is the author of a book on the aesthetics of the object in the poetry of João Cabral and of numerous articles on poetry and gender in Brazilian literature.

www.ingramcontent.com/pod-product-compliance
Lightning Source LLC
Chambersburg PA
CBHW061416300426
44114CB00015B/1958